Anonymous

Ritual conformity

Interpretations of the rubrics of the prayer-book

Anonymous

Ritual conformity
Interpretations of the rubrics of the prayer-book

ISBN/EAN: 9783337225124

Printed in Europe, USA, Canada, Australia, Japan

Cover: Foto ©Lupo / pixelio.de

More available books at **www.hansebooks.com**

RITUAL CONFORMITY.

INTERPRETATIONS

OF THE

RUBRICS OF THE PRAYER-BOOK,

AGREED UPON BY A CONFERENCE HELD
AT ALL SAINTS, MARGARET-STREET, 1880—1881.

PARKER AND CO.

OXFORD, AND 6 SOUTHAMPTON-STREET,
STRAND, LONDON.

1881.

PREFACE.

A T a Conference of some friends interested in the subject of Ritual, held on January 17, 1880, the following propositions were, amongst others, agreed to :—

I. That the evil of unnecessary Diversity in Ritual, as practised in various Churches aiming at the maintenance of Catholic doctrine and usage in the Church of England, is real and great.

II. That an effort to moderate it should be attempted, resting mainly on the united opinion of some of those who have given special attention to the theory and practice of Ritual, in their private capacity of Students or Parish Priests.

III. That the effort should take the form of a body of Comments upon the Rubrics of the Book of Common Prayer, and that these Comments should include cautions against practices which are infractions of the law and usage of the Church of England.

With the view of carrying these propositions into effect, it was arranged that a series of meetings should be held ; and the Vicar of All Saints, Margaret-street, kindly provided a room at the clergy-house for the meetings of the Conference.

Those who had met in the first instance were duly summoned, and others were invited to join them. The meetings were held at first on two consecutive days in alternate weeks, (since some of the members came from a considerable distance). Latterly, in order to expedite the work, meetings were held on three consecutive days in alternate weeks. In all, forty-eight meetings were held between January 17, 1880, and July 13, 1881.

It was thought possible that by the co-operation of several minds, information might be collected from sources not com-

monly accessible, and perhaps hardly within the reach of any
one individual. Among the members of the Conference also
were those who had had experience of parish-work, as well
as those who had devoted time and attention to historical
enquiry into the origin and meaning of the Rubrics of the
Prayer-Book, or who had made ancient Liturgies their special
study : some, it may be added, combined these various quali-
fications. A hope therefore was entertained, as the second
proposition implies, that by considering on very wide grounds
(both practical and historical), and not from any one point of
view, the various divergencies of ritual practice, some agreement might be arrived at even on the most controverted
points.

This hope has been realized. It was found that points
which seemed at first to afford no basis on which agreement
was at all probable, were settled, after long discussion, almost
(if not quite) unanimously; but this involved expenditure of
time, and much investigation into matters on which existing
text-books were often silent.

With regard to the actual diversities in ritual which came
under the attention of the Conference, some appeared to be
such direct infractions of the Rubrics that no explanation of
the Rubrics could make their irregularity more evident.
Others seemed to arise from well-meant attempts to interpret
the Rubrics. These last formed the chief subject of the la-
bours of the Conference.

The main line of procedure laid down was a true and loyal
adherence to the spirit of the Prayer-Book. A mere literal
interpretation of the Rubric was found in many cases to be
insufficient. Even if the existing Prayer-Book had been com-
posed for inaugurating some new religious system, it would
be scarcely reasonable to depend upon the abstract meaning of the words employed, without any reference to the
circumstances under which the book had been written. But
when we remember that the Prayer-Book of 1662 was the last

of several revisions of the original English Prayer-Book of 1549, which was itself avowedly based upon the Ancient Liturgies, and carried on the existing and ancient worship of the Church of England (with such reformation as was considered needful), no mode of interpretation could be more misleading if rigorously insisted on, or so likely to cause error in practice.

The Prayer-Book, however, in spite of the Revision of 1662, retains many vestiges of the foreign Protestant influence, which affected the Revision of 1552. With these the Conference have attempted to deal in a loyal spirit. However much they may be regretted, Churchmen are bound to accept them. For it must be clearly understood that nothing was further from the intention of the Conference, than to attempt Revision. So far from this, it was hoped by some that a careful series of notes explaining the true character of disputed Rubrics might go some way to allay the present agitation for change.

The Conference cannot be blind to the conviction that they have to face much modern prejudice. On the one hand there is still rife in the Church of England the Puritan spirit, which condemns in one and the same category things essentially Roman, and things which are really primitive, but which have been retained by Rome. On the other hand, there undoubtedly exists an occasional reaction from this Puritan spirit, which has produced a prejudice in favour of things —whether primitive or not—simply because they are Roman. The Conference have felt that to yield either to one or the other prejudice was not the right way of dealing with the Prayer-Book.

They have also been brought face to face with what are called "Legal decisions" on some questions of Ritual. Apart from the fact that the courts have given directly opposite decisions on the same question, and have given reasons in one case inconsistent with the reasons given for their decision in another; apart also from the fact that these are chiefly decisions of secular courts in purely spiritual matters; the Conference have been precluded from entertaining them, as guides or as helps, in consequence of the courts having generally acted upon principles of interpretation entirely different from those which the Conference had adopted.

They have, moreover, found themselves in opposition to much modern practice, originating in carelessness and neglect in the due performance of the Services of the Church during past generations, but alien to the spirit of those Services, though often mistaken for their exponent.

The Conference have had to investigate the origin and to consider the meaning of many practices, which appear either to be enjoined or implied in the existing Rubrics, and have, in the light of these investigations, set down unflinchingly what they believed to be the true interpretation of these Rubrics. At the same time, they have not shut their eyes to ancient customs, which, though less prominently connected with the Rubrics, appear to have held on concurrently with the Prayer-Book; being consistent with its principles, and not authoritatively condemned either by name or by implication.

The Comments, which have been the result of their discussions, the Conference have printed, in the hope that they will be received by others as suggestions towards the solution of difficulties which must press upon all who desire to obey the spirit as well as the letter of the Prayer-Book.

The entire adherence of any one to all the interpretations here offered is not to be expected. Indeed, those members of the Conference who have had experience in parish-work, are well aware that in comparatively few villages it is possible to carry out the fuller Ritual which the Prayer-Book admits: this can only be successfully adopted in large towns, or where endowments are provided, or other resources are available, for sustaining a high Ritual.

It should be said, in conclusion, that amongst the members of the Conference, some have taken part in the work to a greater extent than others, and are consequently more directly responsible for the Comments, and able to give a fuller assent to them. It was impossible to consult every member upon each individual point. All that was done to ensure the expression of the general sense of the Conference, was to determine to insert no comment which was not approved of by two-thirds of the members present. Practically, it was found that in very few cases a formal division was called for, the agreement to the final form of the comments being generally unanimous.

(*Signed,*)

B. COMPTON, *Chairman.*

WM. JNO. BLEW.	H. G. MORSE.
J. H. BLUNT.	JAMES PARKER.
WM. COOKE.	THOS. W. PERRY.
C. L. COURTENAY.	JAMES BADEN POWELL.
J. FULLER RUSSELL.	R. F. WILSON.
R. F. LITTLEDALE.	CHR. WORDSWORTH.

INTERPRETATIONS OF THE RUBRICS OF THE PRAYER-BOOK.

----◆----

THE PREFACE.

1. It hath been the wisdom of the Church of *England*, &c.

IT is important to bear in mind, in interpreting the prefaces and rubrics of the Prayer-Book, that they were written at various times, and that their language is not generally the current language of our own day, but the technical language of the times at which they were respectively written.

The first section, headed " The Preface," was added in 1662 to the second, entitled " Concerning the Service of the Church," which is the original Preface to the Prayer-Book of 1549, with some important additions and slight omissions made in 1552.

The " Order how the Psalter is appointed to be read," dates mainly from 1549.

The " Order how the rest of Holy Scripture is appointed to be read," with the Tables of Proper Psalms, and Lessons, and the Calendar—originally forming part of the book of 1549— was adopted with slight alteration in 1662, but was much varied in 1871.

CONCERNING THE SERVICE OF THE CHURCH.

2. There was never any thing by the wit of man so well devised, &c.

It seems that, having regard to the circumstances under which this rubric was framed, the 'diversity to be appeased,' and the ' doubts to be resolved,' concerned only the manner of saying and singing the Morning and Evening Prayer, not the manner of administration of the Sacraments or other Rites and Ceremonies of the Church. Nor were any 'parties' contemplated as likely to 'doubt, or diversely take anything,' except the clergy. The contemporaneous Latin translation of the English Prayer-Book expressly confines this provision of resort to the Bishop of the diocese to questions arising *inter ministros*. The Bishop of the Diocese was the proper person to resort to, both on account of his sacred office, which gave him authority, and also as being at that time the person likely to be best informed on questions of this kind, as the

B

Epistle, and Gospel for Quinquagesima Sunday (with the addition of the Collect of Ash Wednesday), but the Scotch Prayer-Book directs the use of the Collect, Epistle, and Gospel for Ash Wednesday only; and Bishop Cosin directed the Collect, Epistle, and Gospel for Quinquagesima Sunday to serve only until Ash Wednesday.

When more than one Collect is appointed for the day, by reason of the coincidence of Holy Days, the question arises which Holy Day should take precedence.

Coincidence includes (*a*) occurrence (i.e. the falling on the same day of two occasions having special services), and (*b*) concurrence, when the one falls on the morrow of the other.

By taking precedence is meant, that when two Holy Days occur, the Collect, Epistle, and Gospel, the Proper Psalms and Lessons (if any) of the superior day should be used.

But in certain cases of occurrence, noticed in the following Table, a memorial of the inferior day should be made, by using the Collect appointed for it in addition to, and after, the Collect for the superior day, at all services at which the Collect for the day is to be said.

In other cases, the services of the inferior day must be entirely omitted for that year, or transferred to the morrow, or some subsequent date, in accordance with ancient custom. The Prayer-Book gives no directions for such transference, but the total loss for the year of such Festivals as the Annunciation of the Blessed Virgin, or of the Dedication and the Title of a Church, would be much to be regretted.

The following Table exhibits the precedence of Holy Days :—

First Sunday in Advent takes precedence of St. Andrew's Day.

Fourth Sunday in Advent takes precedence of St. Thomas' Day.

St. Stephen's Day
St. John the Evangelist's Day } take precedence of First
Holy Innocents' Day } Sunday after Christmas.
The Circumcision

The Epiphany takes precedence of Second Sunday after Christmas.

The Conversion of St. Paul takes precedence of Third Sunday after Epiphany, but memorial is to be made of the Sunday.

The Purification takes precedence of Fourth Sunday after Epiphany, also of Septuagesima, Sexagesima, Quinquagesima Sundays, of which three Sundays memorial is to be made.

Septuagesima, Sexagesima, and Quinquagesima Sundays take precedence of Conversion of St. Paul and St. Matthias' Day.

Ash Wednesday takes precedence of St. Matthias' Day.

Third, Fourth, Fifth, and Sixth Sundays in Lent take precedence of the Annunciation.

The services of the season from Evening Prayer on Wednesday in Holy Week till Saturday in Easter Week, both inclusive, take precedence of the Annunciation.

First Sunday after Easter takes precedence of the Annunciation, St. Mark's Day, and SS. Philip and James' Day.

St. Mark's Day, SS. Philip and James' Day } take precedence of Second, Third, Fourth, and Fifth Sundays after Easter.

Ascension Day takes precedence of SS. Philip and James' Day.

The Services of the season from Whitsun Eve till Saturday in Whitsun Week, both inclusive, take precedence of St. Barnabas' Day.

Trinity Sunday takes precedence of St. Barnabas' Day.

St. Barnabas' Day, the Nativity of St. John the Baptist, St. Peter's Day, St. James' Day, St. Bartholomew's Day, St. Matthew's Day, St. Michael and All Angels' Day, St. Luke's Day, SS. Simon and Jude's Day, All Saints' Day, take precedence of all Sundays after Trinity.

The Feasts of the Dedication and Title of a Church rank as principal festivals; but may not be observed on Advent Sunday, Christmas Eve, Christmas Day, Epiphany, between the Fifth Sunday in Lent and Low Sunday inclusive, Ascension Day, or from Whitsun Eve to Trinity Sunday inclusive.

Octaves are not mentioned by name in the Prayer-Book, but are implied in the rubrics preceding the Proper Prefaces of the Communion Office. It has been suggested by the Convocation of Canterbury that the Collects for St. Michael's and All Saints' Days should be repeated on the seven days following those days respectively. Such additions would be in the nature of new Octaves. But the first of these days had no Octave in the Sarum or the Roman Use: the second has an Octave in the Roman Use, but had none in the

Sarum Use.   If any such additional Octaves are introduced, the Festival of the Epiphany at least should have this distinction.   A general permission might also be given to individual churches to keep the Octaves of their title or dedication.

7. *PROPER LESSONS*

To be read at Morning and Evening Prayer, on the Sundays, and other Holy-days throughout the Year.

LESSONS PROPER FOR HOLY-DAYS.

8. *PROPER PSALMS ON CERTAIN DAYS.*

9. *THE CALENDAR, WITH THE TABLE OF LESSONS.*

The Black-letter days, especially those that commemorate Scriptural persons and events, should be observed if possible. They may be marked by sermons and suitable hymns.

10. *TABLES AND RULES*

For the Moveable and Immoveable Feasts ; together with the Days of Fasting and Abstinence, through the whole Year.

11. *RULES* to know when the Moveable Feasts and Holy-days begin.

12. *A TABLE* of all the Feasts that are to be observed in the Church of England throughout the Year.

All Sundays in the Year.

The Days of the Feasts of
- The Circumcision of our Lord JESUS CHRIST.
- The Epiphany.
- The Conversion of S. *Paul.*
- The Purification of the Blessed Virgin.
- S. *Matthias* the Apostle.
- The Annunciation of the Blessed Virgin.
- S. *Mark* the Evangelist.
- S. *Philip* and S. *James* the Apostles.
- The Ascension of our Lord JESUS CHRIST.
- S. *Barnabas.*
- The Nativity of S. *John* Bapt.

The Days of the Feasts of
- S. *Peter* the Apostle.
- S. *James* the Apostle.
- S. *Bartholomew* the Apostle.
- S. *Matthew* the Apostle.
- S. *Michael* and all Angels.
- S. *Luke* the Evangelist.
- S. *Simon* and S. *Jude*, Apostles.
- All Saints.
- S. *Andrew* the Apostle.
- S. *Thomas* the Apostle.
- The Nativity of our Lord.
- S. *Stephen* the Martyr.
- S. *John* the Evangelist.
- The Holy Innocents.

Monday and *Tuesday* in *Easter-week*.   *Monday* and *Tuesday* in *Whitsun-week.*

13. *A TABLE* of the Vigils, Fasts, and Days of Abstinence, to be observed in the Year.

The Evens or Vigils before	The Nativity of our Lord. The Purification of the Blessed Virgin *Mary*. The Annunciation of the Blessed Virgin. Easter-Day. Ascension-Day. Pentecost. S. *Matthias*.	The Evens or Vigils before	S. *John Baptist.* S. *Peter.* S. *James.* S. *Bartholomew.* S. *Matthew.* S. *Simon* and S. *Jude.* S. *Andrew.* S. *Thomas.* All Saints.

Note, That if any of these Feast-Days fall upon a *Monday*, then the Vigil or Fast-Day shall be kept upon the *Saturday*, and not upon the *Sunday* next before it.

This Table includes several days not anciently observed as Fast-days, and refers to private observance and not to public service.

When a Saint's Day which is preceded by a Vigil falls on a Monday, though the fast of the Vigil is to be kept on the Saturday, yet the Collect for the Saint's Day is not to be said on the Saturday evening, but on the evening of Sunday, in accordance with Rubric (82).

DAYS of Fasting, or Abstinence.

I. The Forty Days of Lent.
II. The Ember-Days at the Four Seasons, being the *Wednesday, Friday,* and *Saturday* after { The First *Sunday* in Lent. The Feast of *Pentecost. September* 14, and *December* 13.
III. The Three *Rogation-Days*, being the *Monday, Tuesday,* and *Wednesday,* before *Holy Thursday*, or the *Ascension* of our LORD.
IV. All the *Fridays* in the Year, except CHRISTMAS-DAY.

The word 'or' implies a distinction in the mode of observing these days : Nos. I. and II. in the 'Table,' viz., the Forty Days of Lent and the Ember-days, are days of *Fasting :* Nos. III. and IV., viz., the three Rogation-days and Fridays, except Christmas-Day, are days of *Abstinence.*

14. *A CERTAIN SOLEMN DAY,* for which a particular Service is appointed.

The Twentieth Day of *June,* being the Day on which her Majesty began her happy Reign.

MORNING AND EVENING PRAYER

15. The Morning and Evening Prayer shall be used in the accustomed Place of the Church, Chapel, or Chancel; except it shall be otherwise determined by the Ordinary of the Place. And the Chancels shall remain as they have done in times past.

The direction given in the first clause of this rubric was introduced in 1559, in correction of the order of 1552, which had enabled the Minister to choose any place in which the people could best hear. It was retained in 1662, and in reading the clause with the second, it appears distinctly to point to the ancient use, when the accustomed place for the minister was within the chancel.

The direction that the Chancels shall remain as in times past, dates from 1552, and must therefore refer to arrangements before that time. It seems also definitely to refer to the retaining the screen, and the steps, as interpreted by the order of 1561. Hence no fixtures may be introduced, such as pews, monuments, &c., nor any alteration made in the furniture or ornaments of the Chancels, which will interfere with the convenience of the Minister and Clerks in the celebration of Holy Communion, or other offices of the Church.

16. And here is to be noted, that such Ornaments of the Church, and of the Ministers thereof, at all Times of their Ministration, shall be retained, and be in use, as were in this Church of *England*, by the Authority of Parliament, in the Second Year of the Reign of King *Edward* the Sixth.

This paragraph of the rubric is essentially taken from the Act of Uniformity of 1559. In the ecclesiastical language of that day, the word 'ornaments' technically includes everything which is connected with the purposes of the consecrated building beyond the mere fabric of the building, and with the dress of the officiating Minister beyond his usual dress in secular life.

In the Act of 1559, the intention was to take as the basis of the Prayer-Book then authorized the Book of the fifth and sixth years of Edward VI. (1552); but to adopt the ornaments of another period, viz. of the second, not of the fifth year of Edward VI.[b]

The ornaments of the second year are those which were intended to be, and were actually, used under the Prayer-Book of 1549. Whatever question may arise about other ornaments, there can be no question about those prescribed by that Book, as well as those implied in it. As to those which were not prescribed by, or implied in, that book, they must be determined by the existing usage of the time, subject to such mo-

---

[b] "The Act of Uniformity is to be construed by the same rules exactly as any act passed in the last session of Parliament. The clause in question, by which I mean the rubric in question (the Ornaments Rubric), is perfectly unambiguous in language, free from all difficulty as to construction. It therefore lets in no argument as to intention other than that which the words themselves import. There might be a seeming difficulty in fact, because it might not be known what vestments were in use by authority of Parliament in the second year of the reign of King Edward the Sixth; but this difficulty has been removed. It is conceded in the report that the vestments, the use of which is now condemned, were in use by authority of Parliament in that year. Having that fact, you are bound to construe the rubric as if those vestments were specifically named in it, instead of being only referred to. If an act should be passed to-morrow that the uniform of the Guards should henceforth be such as was ordered for them by authority, and used by them in the 1st George I., you would first ascertain what that uniform was, and having ascertained it, you would not enquire into the changes which may have been made, many or few, with or without lawful authority, between the 1st George I. and the passing of the new act. All these, from that act specifying the earlier date, would have been made wholly immaterial. It would have seemed strange, I suppose, if a commanding officer, disobeying the statute, had said in his defence, 'There have been many changes since the reign of George I., and as to "retaining," we put a gloss on that, and thought it might mean only retaining to the Queen's use; so we have put the uniforms safely in store.' But I think it would have seemed more strange to punish and mulct him severely, if he had obeyed the law and put no gloss on plain words.

"This case stands on the same principle. The rubric, indeed, seems to me to imply with some clearness that, in the long interval between Edw. VI. and the 14th Car. II., there had been many changes; but it does not stay to specify them, or distinguish between what was mere evasion, and what was lawful. It quietly passes them all by, and goes back to *the legalized usage of the second year of Edward VI.* What had prevailed since, whether by an archbishop's gloss, by commissioners, or even statutes, whether, in short, legal or illegal, it makes quite immaterial."—*Remarks on some parts of the Report of the Judicial Committee in the case of Elphinstone v. Purchas, and on the course proper to be pursued by the Clergy in regard to it.* A Letter to the Rev. Canon Liddon from the Right Hon. J. T. Coleridge. (1871.)

difications as were implied by the Injunctions, or other authoritative documents, up to the year 1548.

The following ornaments are prescribed by the Book of 1549.

1. Altar.	9. Surplice.
2. Chalice.	10. Hood.
3. Paten.	11. Albe.
4. Corporas.	12. Vestment[c].
5. Font.	13. Tunicle.
6. Poor Man's Box.	14. Rochet.
7. Bell.	15. Cope.
8. Pulpit.	16. Pastoral Staff.

This rubric, if construed to include only these ornaments, would exclude many things which common sense and custom have sanctioned; and if the doctrine that "omission is prohibition" be insisted on, would actually shut out organs or harmoniums, hangings on doorways, seats for priests, clerks, and people, stoves, hassocks, pulpit-cloths or pulpit-cushions, pews, Christmas decorations, and the use of the pulpit or bell except on Ash Wednesday; it would forbid any bishop to officiate publicly on any occasion without a cope or vestment and pastoral staff. On the other hand, there seems to be a limit to laxity in construing the rubric, and that it cannot, unless this laxity be strained beyond the bounds of reason, be taken to admit the substitution of other ornaments for those which the rubric enjoins; such as the use of a bason in, or instead of the Church font, of a common bottle for the Holy Communion, of a black gown instead of an authorised vesture in the pulpit during the Communion Service, or of foreign forms of surplices and vestments instead of the English ones.

In general, the more nearly the ornaments of the Church and Minister, and the use thereof, are conformed to the English usage in the early years of the reign of Edward VI., the better; as marking the continuity of the English Church, and avoiding the imputation of adopting at second hand the ornaments and usages of foreign communions, whether Belgian, French, Italian, or Swiss.

Nevertheless, the non-user of any legal ornaments, such as the Eucharistic Vestments, in any old Church, for a long

---

[c] We gather from the Inventories and other authorities, that the word *vestment* generally included, besides the chasuble, the stole and maniple, and the albe with its amice and girdle.

period, seems to be a valid plea against any absolute obligation
of sudden restoration in that Church, when the communicants
do not desire them to be restored.

With regard to the colours of the Priest's vestments, and of
other coloured ornaments of the Church and Minister, there
were variations in different Churches.

In the rubric of Sarum, which seems to have been regarded as a standard of English usage up to the beginning
of the reign of Edward VI., *red* was directed to be used on
all Sundays in the year, except in the Easter season and
the Ascension festival (up to Whitsun Eve), and except on
any other festival marked by the use of white, which takes
precedence of the particular Sunday. In these cases the
colour would be *white*.

Also on the Circumcision the colour would be White.

On the Epiphany	,,	,,	White.
On the Conversion of St. Paul	,,	White.
On the Purification	,,	,,	White.
On St. Matthias' Day	,,	,,	Red.
On the Annunciation	,,	,,	White.
On St. Mark's Day	,,	,,	White (because in Easter Season).
On St. Philip and St. James' Day	,,	
On the Ascension	,,	,,	White.
On St. Barnabas' Day	,,	,,	Red (White if in Easter Season).
On St. John the Baptist's Day	,,	White.
On St. Peter's Day	,,	,,	Red.
On St. James' Day	,,	,,	Red.
On St. Bartholomew's Day	,,	Red.
On St. Matthew's Day	,,	,,	Red.
On St. Michael and All Angels'	,,	White.
On St. Luke's Day	,,	,,	Red.
On St. Simon and St. Jude's Day	,,	Red.
On All Saints' Day	,,	,,	Red.
On St. Andrew's Day	,,	,,	Red.
On St. Thomas' Day	,,	,,	Red.
In the Christmas Season	,,	,,	White (probably).
On St. Stephen's Day	,,	,,	Red.
On St. John the Evangelist's Day		White.
On Holy Innocents' Day	,,	Red.
On the Festival of the Dedication of the Church		White.

On Week-days the colour generally followed the colour of the Sunday or other day, the Communion Office of which was used.

The inventories, however, of many Churches made in the middle of the sixteenth century shew that numerous colours were in use, such as blue, green, black, and others (many of which it is difficult to reconcile with any known ritual). In their use, regard was probably had rather to their comparative splendour than to their colour.

The rubrics of 1549, 1559, and 1662 did not disturb them. And therefore, although neither law nor custom recognise the modern Roman sequence of colours, still there is precedent for the use of colours not specified in the rubric of Sarum, on days not mentioned therein, especially in Churches which already possess them.

THE ORDER FOR MORNING PRAYER,

17. *Daily throughout the Year.*

In coming into Church (as in going out of the same, and in going up to, and coming down from the altar) obeisance is made by the minister as an ancient and devout usage [d].

---

[d] "'To bow reverently at 'the name of Jesus' whenever it is mentioned in any of the Church's offices; to turn towards the East when the *Gloria Patri* and Creeds are rehearsing; and to make obeisance at coming into and going out of Church; and at going up to, and coming down from, the altar, are all ancient and devout usages, and which thousands of good people of our own Church practise at this day, and amongst them, if he deserves to be reckoned among them, T. W.'s good friend."—*Michael Hewetson's Memorandums concerning the Consecration of the Church of Kildare, and the Ordination of his dear friend, Thomas Wilson* [S. Peter's-day, 1686], *with some Advices thereon.* Quoted in Life of Bishop Wilson, edited by the Rev. John Keble. A.-C.L., Part I. cap. i. p. 22.

"Whereas the Church is the house of God, dedicated to his holy worship, and therefore ought to mind us both of the greatnesse and goodness of his Divine Majestie, certain it is that the acknowledgement thereof not onely inwardly in our hearts, but also outwardly with our bodies, must needs be pious in itself, profitable unto us, and edifying unto others. We therefore think it very meet and behovefull, and heartily commend it to all good and well-affected people members of this Church, that they be ready to tender unto the Lord the said acknowledgement, by doing reverence and obeisance both at their coming in and going out of the said churches, chancels, or chapels, according to the most ancient custome of the Primitive Church in the purest times, and of the Church also for many yeers of the reign of Queen Elizabeth."—*The Canons of the Church of England,* 1640, No. vii.

18. At the beginning of Morning Prayer the Minister shall read with a loud voice some one or more of these Sentences of the Scriptures that follow. And then he shall say that which is written after the said Sentences.

Two terms are here used, viz., 'read with a loud voice,' and 'say.' The words 'a loud voice' have been continued in the opening rubric of the service since 1549, when the Priest was directed to 'begin with a loud voice the Lord's Prayer,' which previously had been said '*secreto.*' In 1552, when the office was arranged to begin with the Sentences, they were ordered to be 'read with a loud voice.'

That 'read' may mean a musical recital, whether monotone or inflected, can be inferred from the rubric of the lessons which existed in the Prayer-Book from 1549 to 1604. " Then shall be *read* two Lessons distinctly with a loud voice, that the people may hear. . . . And, to the end that the people may *better* hear, in such places where they do sing, there shall the Lessons be *sung* in a plain tune after the manner of distinct reading, and likewise the Epistle and Gospel." The 'Ministers' in 1661 took 'Exceptions' to this rubric on the ground that this portion of the Service " being for the most part neither Psalms nor Hymns, we know no warrant why they should be sung in any place, and conceive that the distinct reading of them with an audible voice tends more to the edification of the Church." To this the bishops replied, that "the rubric directs only such singing as is after the manner of distinct reading, and we never heard of any inconvenience thereby, and therefore conceive this demand to be needless."

The latter portion of this rubric, explaining the most effectual manner of distinct reading, was indeed omitted in 1662 ; but, though the Lessons, Epistle, and Gospel are no longer *required* to be 'sung' anywhere, the word 'read' must have included that manner of reading when directed for the Sentences in 1552.

The word 'say' was applied to the Exhortation, 'Dearly beloved,' &c., when that was introduced in 1552, and has been continued ever since. It occurs in the rubric before the versicles after the first Lord's Prayer (No. 23, below), viz., 'Then likewise shall he say,' dating from 1549, where the word 'likewise' indicated that the word 'begin' in the preceding rubric of that book meant 'say.' And if the word

'likewise' had been used in the latter portion of this rubric,
'read' must have been also interpreted to be identical with
'say.' But it is not used here, and therefore, the word 'read'
need not mean the same as the word 'say;' and, consequently,
while 'say' strictly means a monotone (as distinct from 'sing,'
which implies inflections); 'read' includes some other mode
of reciting the Sentences, such as singing.

This rubric does not give any direction as to the posture
or position of the Minister at the Sentences and Exhortation. But the next rubric implies standing to be the pos-
ture; while his position is indicated in the answer of the
Bishops to the Ministers in the Savoy Conference, "The
Minister turning to the people is not most convenient throughout the whole ministration. When he speaks to them, as in
Lessons, Absolution, and Benediction, it is convenient that
he turn to them." The Exhortation falls under this class.
Further, the Bishops said, "When he speaks for them to
God, it is fit they should all turn another way, as the Ancient
Church ever did." But the Sentences are not in the nature
of prayer; therefore, the Minister in reading them would
seem to be correct if he stood 'stall-wise,' as he would in
complying with the order that 'the chancels shall remain as
they have done in times past.'

In selecting the particular Sentences for use at certain
seasons it seems suitable to use

in Advent,	'Repent ye,' &c.
in Lent,	'Rend your hearts,' &c.
	And the Sentences from Ps. 51.
on Sundays and Festivals,	'To the Lord our God,' &c.,
	'I will arise,' &c.
on Week-days,	'Enter not into judgment,' &c.

The other Sentences can be used at any time.

19. A general Confession to be said of the whole Congregation after
the Minister, all kneeling. Almighty and most merciful Father, &c.

The epithet 'general' prefixed to the word 'Confession'
mainly refers to the generality of its expressions, as being said
by the whole congregation, and not being individual or particular. It was ordered to be said not 'with' but 'after' the
Minister—i.e. each clause, as marked by an initial capital,
should be completely said by the Minister, and then repeated
by the congregation. This was probably because the congregation required to be taught it, it being new in 1552.

The phrase 'humble voice,' in the closing Sentence of the preceding Exhortation, seems to have a double force, moral and vocal ; and to point to the careful solemnity with which the Confession should be said. A low pitch of voice, therefore, such as is easily within the reach of all, and a moderately slow time, seem absolutely necessary.

In Musical Services it is best to recite on E rather than on G or A, to the end of the Lord's Prayer, dropping a third to C, as customary, at 'O Lord, open Thou our lips,' and rising to G at 'Glory be to the Father,' &c. On this point it should be remembered that the standard musical pitch three centuries ago—i.e. in the time of Marbeck and Tallis—was considerably. lower than the present standard pitch.

20. The Absolution, or Remission of sins, to be pronounced by the Priest alone, standing; the people still kneeling. Almighty God, &c.

Of late years, Bishops, when present at Morning Prayer, have sometimes pronounced this Absolution instead of the Priest who is officiating. But the absence of any such direction as that which is given in the Communion Office appears to shew that this practice was not intended at Morning or Evening Prayer.

A Deacon, officiating in the absence of a Priest, may not use this Absolution as a prayer, nor may he substitute for it either the prayer, 'O God, whose nature,' &c., or any other prayer.

21. The people shall answer here, and at the end of all other prayers, Amen.

Amen is a ratification of what has preceded, sometimes by the speaker himself, as in S. John v. 24, 25, vi. 53, Rom. ix. 5 ; sometimes by the hearers, as in Deut. xxvii. 15, &c., Psalm cvi. 48, 1 Cor. xiv. 16. When used at the conclusion of parts of Divine Service in which the Minister and people join aloud, as in Confessions, Creeds, the Lord's Prayer, and Doxologies, it will be said, as part of the devotion itself, by both Minister and people. When used after acts of worship in which the Minister only has spoken, as in Absolutions, Benedictions, and 'other prayers' said by the minister alone, it is an answer of the people, and therefore to be said by the people only.

In the Lord's Prayer at the beginning of the Communion Office, and in the formulæ of Baptism, and of reception into the Church, it is a ratification by the speaker himself, not an answer of the people, and should not, as it seems, be said by the people also.

22. Then the Minister shall kneel, and say the Lord's Prayer with an audible voice; the people also kneeling, and repeating it with him, both here, and wheresoever else it is used in Divine Service.

The Lord's Prayer is to be repeated by the people with, not after the Minister, i.e., taking up each clause as he begins it, in the same manner as the Creed. It was ordered in 1549, 1552, and 1604, that the Priest [Minister] should begin the Lord's Prayer. This is a reason for the practice of the Priest saying the first two words alone.

23. Then likewise he shall say, O Lord, open, &c.
24. Here all standing up, the Priest shall say, Glory be, &c.

The posture of standing, here directed, is to be continued through the *Venite* and Psalms. It is a devout usage to turn to the East at the *Gloria Patri*. (See *ante*, p. 12, note d.)

It is also an old custom in some places to bow.

25. Then shall be said or sung this Psalm following : except on *Easter-Day*, upon which another Anthem is appointed; and on the Nineteenth day of every Month it is not to be read here, but in the ordinary Course of the Psalms. O come, let us sing, &c.

With regard to Easter Day, it is to be noticed that the "other anthem" provided for that day is intended to be used on that day only and not during the Octave, in accordance with the ancient precedent of using on Easter Day only the short Introductory Office in which the central part and foundation of the Anthem (viz. ' Christ being raised,' &c.) occurred. If it be desired, therefore, to use this group of Anthems during the remainder of Easter Week, it must be sung as an Anthem after the third collect, but it should not be substituted for the *Venite*.

26. Then shall follow the Psalms in order as they are appointed. And at the end of every Psalm throughout the Year, and likewise at the end of *Benedicite, Benedictus, Magnificat,* and *Nunc dimittis,* shall be repeated,

This rubric forbids the substitution of any selected Psalms for those of the day, other than those appointed in the Table of Proper Psalms. The only exception to this rule is made by the recent provision, in the Order how the rest of Holy Scripture is appointed to be read, viz. " Upon occasions to be appointed by the Ordinary, other Psalms may, with his consent, be substituted for those appointed in the Psalter."

27. Then shall be read distinctly with an audible voice the First Lesson, taken out of the Old Testament, as is appointed in the Calendar, except there be proper Lessons assigned for that day : He that readeth so standing and turning himself, as he may best be heard of all such as are present. And after that, shall be said or sung, in *English*, the Hymn called *Te Deum Laudamus*, daily throughout the Year.

The order to 'read distinctly and with an audible voice so as best to be heard of all such as are present,' is an essential part of this rubric, and enjoins that careful attention should be paid to the accurate enunciation of the words and to adequate loudness of voice. It must be remembered that the variety of Scripture lessons makes this the more important, as the people cannot be supposed to be equally familiar with all.

The direction to the reader to turn, indicates a change from the previous position, specially appropriate to prayer and praise, and a transition to a part of the Service intended to teach, and, therefore, directly addressed to the people. The expression, 'and turning himself as he may best be heard,' justifies his going to the chancel entrance, or into the nave of the church, and reading there, with or without the use of a lectern.

The alternative between the use of the *Te Deum* and *Benedicite* may be governed by the direction given in the Prayer-Book of 1549, viz. to use *Te Deum* " daily throughout the year, except in Lent, all which time in place of *Te Deum* shall be used *Benedicite*."

28. Note, That before every Lesson the Minister shall say, *Here beginneth such a Chapter*, or *Verse of such a Chapter, of such a Book;* And after every Lesson, *Here endeth the First*, or *the Second Lesson*.

29. Or this Canticle, *Benedicite, &c.*

30. Then shall be read in like manner the Second Lesson, taken out of the New Testament. And after that, the Hymn following ; except when that shall happen to be read in the Chapter for the Day, or for the Gospel on *St. John Baptist's* Day.

No liberty is here given for the omission of the Benedictus at any other times than those here specified, viz. "when it shall be read in the chapter for the day, or for the Gospel on S. John Baptist's day."

31. Or this Psalm, *Jubilate Deo, &c.*

32. Then shall be sung or said the Apostles' Creed by the Minister and the people, standing : except only such days as the Creed of Saint *Athanasius* is appointed to be read. I believe, &c.

When the Name of the Lord JESUS is pronounced, the inclination of the head should not be neglected, nor superseded by any other gesture; it being the ancient English usage, directed by the 18th Canon to be continued as the accustomed form of due and lowly reverence to the Holy Name.

33. And after that, these Prayers following, all devoutly kneeling; the Minister first pronouncing with a loud voice, The Lord, &c.

The mutual salutation is to be said, both Priest and people standing; the people kneeling down while the Priest says, 'Let us pray.'

34. Then the Minister, Clerks, and people, shall say the Lord's Prayer with a loud voice.

35. Then the Priest standing up shall say, O Lord, shew, &c.

36. Then shall follow three Collects; the first of the Day, which shall be the same that is appointed at the Communion; the second for Peace; the third for Grace to live well. And the two last Collects shall never alter, but daily be said at Morning Prayer throughout all the Year, as followeth; all kneeling.

The number of Collects is fixed at three, as a general rule, to which exceptions are made by other rubrics, as in Lent and Advent, &c. If the Minister uses the discretion of saying, after the Collects of Morning or Evening Prayer, one of the six Collects provided at the end of the Order of Holy Communion, it is proper to say it before the two invariable Collects.

A comparison of other rubrics in the Prayer-Book shews that the words 'all kneeling,' often apply to the congregation only, to the exclusion of the Minister; and as the universal rule up to 1662 was that the officiant, if a Priest, should stand for the Versicles and Collects, it is probable that such is the interpretation of this direction, especially as it is absent from the corresponding place at Evening Prayer.

37. In Quires and Places where they sing, here followeth the Anthem.

The expression 'Quires and Places where they sing,' does not at the present time exclude village churches; but the anthem (suggesting part-music) may in such churches be replaced by the ordinary hymn.

38. Then these five Prayers following are to be read here, except when the Litany is read; and then only the two last are to be read, as they are there placed.

The 'two last' of these prayers are not to be read at Morning Prayer on Litany days, inasmuch as they are then read in the Litany, instead of at Morning Prayer.

39. Here endeth the Order of Morning Prayer throughout the Year.

THE ORDER FOR
EVENING PRAYER,

DAILY THROUGHOUT THE YEAR.

See notes on the Rubrics of Morning Prayer for the corresponding Rubrics of Evening Prayer.

40. At the beginning of Evening Prayer the Minister shall read with a loud voice some one or more of these Sentences of the Scriptures that follow. And then he shall say that which is written after the said Sentences.

41. A general Confession to be said of the whole Congregation after the Minister, all kneeling.

42. The Absolution, or Remission of sins, to be pronounced by the Priest alone, standing ; the people still kneeling.

43. Then the Minister shall kneel, and say the Lord's Prayer ; the people also kneeling, and repeating it with him.

44. Then likewise he shall say, O Lord, open, &c.

45. Here all standing up, the Priest shall say, Glory be, &c.

46. Then shall be said or sung the Psalms in order as they are appointed. Then a Lesson of the Old Testament, as is appointed. And after that, *Magnificat* (or the Song of the blessed Virgin *Mary*) in English, as followeth.

47. Or else this Psalm ; except it be on the Nineteenth Day of the Month, when it is read in the ordinary Course of the Psalms.

48. Then a Lesson of the New Testament, as it is appointed. And after that, *Nunc dimittis* (or the Song of *Symeon*) in English, as followeth.

49. Or else this Psalm ; except it be on the Twelfth Day of the Month.

When Evening Prayer is said once only in the day, it is better never to drop the *Magnificat* or *Nunc Dimittis*. When Evening Prayer is said twice on the same day, it seems proper not to drop the *Magnificat* at the first service (representing the ancient Evensong or Vespers, of which *Magnificat* was an invariable part) ; and, similarly, not to drop the *Nunc Dimittis* at the second service (representing the other component of Evening Prayer, viz. the ancient Compline, at which that Canticle was invariably used), so that in any case one of the Gospel Canticles should be always used.

50. Then shall be said or sung the Apostles' Creed by the Minister and the people, standing.

51. And after that, these Prayers following, all devoutly kneeling ; the Minister first pronouncing with a loud voice, The Lord, &c.

52. Then the Minister, Clerks, and people, shall say the Lord's Prayer with a loud voice.

53. Then the Priest standing up shall say, O Lord, shew, &c.

54. Then shall follow three Collects; the first of the Day; the second for Peace; the third for Aid against all Perils, as hereafter followeth : which two last Collects shall be daily said at Evening Prayer without alteration.

55. In Quires and Places where they sing, here followeth the Anthem.

56. Here endeth the Order of Evening Prayer throughout the Year.

AT MORNING PRAYER.

57. Upon these Feasts ; *Christmas-Day*, the *Epiphany*, Saint *Matthias*, *Easter-Day*, *Ascension-Day*, *Whit-Sunday*, Saint *John Baptist*, Saint *James*, Saint *Bartholomew*, Saint *Matthew*, Saint *Simon* and Saint *Jude*, Saint *Andrew*, and upon *Trinity-Sunday*, shall be sung or said at Morning Prayer, instead of the Apostles' Creed, this Confession of our Christian Faith, commonly called The Creed of Saint *Athanasius*, by the Minister and people standing.

The Athanasian Creed being a Psalm or Hymn, as well as a Confession of Faith, may properly be recited antiphonally as a Psalm, and turning eastward as a Creed.

THE LITANY.

58. Here followeth the LITANY, or General Supplication, to be sung or said after Morning Prayer upon *Sundays*, *Wednesdays*, and *Fridays*, and at other times when it shall be commanded by the Ordinary.

There is no direction in this rubric, as to the place where the Litany is sung or said ; but it is clear from the rubrics of the Commination Service, that it must be distinct from the 'Reading Pew,' or from the place usually occupied by the Minister during Morning and Evening Prayer. From the old Injunctions we learn that it was to be 'in the midst of the church;' in most churches below the chancel-steps. The Minister may exercise his discretion in using a special desk.

In the Injunctions of 1547 and 1559, and in the Communion Office of the Prayer-Book of 1549, the Litany was enjoined to be sung immediately before the Communion. Our present rubric does not insist upon the connexion with the Communion.

The liberty of using it as a separate service, and of combining it with a sermon, or with other services than Morning Prayer, is recognized and confirmed by the Convocations of Canterbury and York, in their report upon which the Act of Uniformity Amendment Act 1872 was framed, enacting the same.

Each of the four opening invocations should be separately sung or said by the people, after it has been completely sung or said by the person officiating. The same should be done with the concluding invocations, 'Son of God,' &c., and with the lesser Litany preceding the Lord's Prayer.

59. Then shall the Priest, and the people with him, say the Lord's Prayer.

60. Here endeth the LITANY.

PRAYERS AND THANKSGIVINGS,

UPON SEVERAL OCCASIONS,

To be used before the two final Prayers of the Litany, or of Morning and Evening Prayer.

PRAYERS.

61. For Rain.

62. For fair Weather.

63. In the time of Dearth and Famine.

64. Or this.

65. In the time of War and Tumults.

66. In the time of any common Plague or Sickness.

67. In the Ember Weeks, to be said every day, for those that are to be admitted into Holy Orders.

68. Or this.

69. A Prayer that may be said after any of the former.

This prayer should ordinarily be reserved for occasions of a penitential character.

70. A Prayer for the High Court of Parliament, to be read during their Session.

71. A Collect or Prayer for all Conditions of men, to be used at such times when the Litany is not appointed to be said.

72. * This to be said when any desire the Prayers of the Congregation. Especially, &c.

It seems most conformable to the rubric to mention the names of those who desire the prayers of the congregation, in substitution for the word 'those' in the parenthesis. But the names, especially when numerous, are commonly given out either before the five prayers at morning or evening prayer, or immediately before this prayer.

THANKSGIVINGS.

The use of the Thanksgivings in the Litany is permitted, when desirable, but is not enjoined.

73. A General Thanksgiving.

The 'General Thanksgiving' for general use, as well as the occasional thanksgivings for occasional use, is to be said by the Minister alone.

74. *This to be said when any that have been prayed for desire to return praise.

It is observable that the words 'return praise,' in contrast with the words 'prayers of the congregation,' in the prayer for all conditions of men, implies the presence of those who desire to return thanks.

75. For Rain.
76. For fair Weather.
77. For Plenty.
78. For Peace and Deliverance from our Enemies.
79. For restoring Publick Peace at Home.
80. For Deliverance from the Plague, or other common Sickness.
81. Or this.

THE COLLECTS, EPISTLES, AND GOSPELS
TO BE USED THROUGHOUT THE YEAR.

82. Note, that the Collect appointed for every Sunday, or for any Holy-day that hath a Vigil or Eve, shall be said at the Evening Service next before.

The Holy-days which have no vigil or eve, and therefore do not fall under this rule, are Ash-Wednesday and Good Friday. The Circumcision, Epiphany, Conversion of St. Paul, St. Mark, St. Philip and St. James, St. Barnabas, St. Michael, St. Luke, have no vigils, but having eves, the Collect is to be said the evening before.

St. Stephen, St. John the Evangelist, and Holy Innocents, have neither vigil nor eve, but the Collects are generally said the evening before, in addition to the proper collect for the day.

THE FIRST SUNDAY IN ADVENT.

83. This Collect is to be repeated every day, with the other Collects in Advent, until Christmas Eve.

SAINT STEPHEN'S DAY.

84. Then shall follow the Collect of the Nativity, which shall be said continually unto New-year's Eve.

THE CIRCUMCISION OF CHRIST.

85. The same Collect, Epistle, and Gospel shall serve for every day after unto the Epiphany.

For the precedence of these Collects, see note on Rubric 6.

The first Day of Lent, commonly called
ASH-WEDNESDAY.

86. This Collect is to be read every day in Lent after the Collect appointed for the Day.

EASTER-DAY.

87. At Morning Prayer, instead of the Psalm, *O come let us sing,* &c. these Anthems shall be sung or said. Christ our passover, &c.

See note on rubric 25, p. 16.

THE TWENTY-FIFTH SUNDAY AFTER TRINITY.

88. If there be any more Sundays before Advent-Sunday, the Service of some of those Sundays that were omitted after the Epiphany shall be taken in to supply so many as are here wanting. And if there be fewer, the overplus may be omitted : Provided that this last Collect, Epistle, and Gospel shall always be used upon the Sunday next before Advent.

If there be twenty-six Sundays after Trinity, the Collect, Epistle, and Gospel for the Sixth Sunday after Epiphany, should be used on the twenty-fifth Sunday. If there be twenty-seven Sundays, the Collect, Epistle, and Gospel for the Fifth Sunday after Epiphany should be used on the twenty-fifth Sunday, and the Collect, Epistle, and Gospel for the Sixth Sunday after Epiphany, on the Twenty-sixth Sunday."

THE ORDER OF THE

ADMINISTRATION OF THE LORD'S SUPPER,

OR

HOLY COMMUNION.

89. So many as intend to be partakers of the holy Communion shall signify their names to the Curate, at least some time the day before.

90. And if any of those be an open and notorious evil liver, or have done any wrcn; to his neighbours by word or deed, so that the Congregation be thereby offended; the Curate, having knowledge thereof, shall call him and advertise him, that in any wise he presume not to come to the Lord's Table, until he hath openly declared himself to have truly repented and amended his former naughty life, that the Congregation may thereby be satisfied, which before were offended; and that he hath recompensed the parties, to whom he hath done wrong; or at least declare himself to be in full purpose so to do, as soon as he conveniently may.

91. The same order shall the Curate use with those betwixt whom he perceiveth malice and hatred to reign ; not suffering them to be partakers of the Lord's Table, until he know them to be reconciled. And if one of the parties so at variance be content to forgive from the bottom of his heart all that the other hath trespassed against him, and to make amends for that he himself hath offended ; and the other party will not be persuaded to a godly unity, but remain still in his frowardness and malice : the Minister in that case ought to admit the penitent person to the holy Communion, and not him that is obstinate. Provided that every Minister so repelling any, as is specified in this, or the next precedent Paragraph of this Rubrick, shall be obliged to give an account of the same to the Ordinary within fourteen days after at the farthest. And the Ordinary shall proceed against the offending person according to the Canon.

The object of this rubric, when introduced in 1549, was to provide some corrective of the lax practice of the unreformed Church in admission of unworthy persons to Communion. In this view, the Curate should be informed of the names of intending Communicants, in order that he may deal with the cases of scandal referred to in the second paragraph, and with the cases of enmity referred to in the third. The main reason of the Church's action herein is the danger of profanation of the Lord's Table by the presence of unworthy Communicants. A second reason is the danger of injury to the consciences of the congregation by wounding their sense of corporate responsibility for individual wrong-doing. A third is the spiritual interest of the offenders themselves, viz., in the words quoted with approval by Hooker (Eccl. Pol. vi. 4—15), "not to strike them with the mortal wound of excommunication, but to stay them rather from running desperately headlong into their own harm, and not to sever from Holy Communion any but such as are either found culpable by their own confession, or have been convicted in some public Court." The mode of the Curate's action was intended by the rubric to be admonition previous and private. The first paragraph indicates the duty of the people, not of the Curate, giving him the opportunity of admonition, but throwing upon them the responsibility of the decision whether or no to present themselves.

The rubric does not empower or entitle the Curate to repel any at the time of Communion, on the *mere* ground of their not having previously signified their names to him. For there is no means provided for receiving their names, or for making any due enquiry; nor is any penalty imposed upon the Curate for communicating people who have not signified their names, nor on the persons who present themselves without having done so. The reference to the Ordinary was added in 1662. The object is to set him in motion as the proper person to take legal proceedings against an offender, and effectually repel one who cannot be repelled by the Curate's weapons of persuasion and admonition.

The precautions of this rubric against communicating unworthily are not very effective, and it must be observed that the 26th, 27th, and 28th Canons extend the Curate's duty in this respect much farther than the rubric, but without giving him any power, which would be recognised by a *secular* Court, of conscientiously performing his duty therein.

92. The Table, at the Communion-time having a fair white linen cloth upon it, shall stand in the Body of the Church, or in the Chancel, where Morning and Evening Prayer are appointed to be said.

The word 'fair,' applied to the white linen cloth in the fourth paragraph of this rubric, means 'beautiful,' and does not exclude adornment with embroidery.

The words 'upon it' require the cloth to lie upon the Mensa, or upper surface of the Table, but do not require the whole Table to be covered or enveloped therewith. The linen cloth is to be laid upon the covering described in Canon 82 as 'a carpet of silk or other decent stuff.'

Bishop Cosin states that "among the Ornaments of the Church that were then (i.e. in the second year of Edward VI.) in use, the setting of two lights upon the Communion Table or Altar was one appointed by the King's Injunctions, set forth about that time, and mentioned or ratified by the Act of Parliament here named (2 & 3 Edw. VI. cap. 1)." If it be contended that Bishop Cosin is wrong in his opinion that the Injunctions were obligatory, we are thrown back upon the universal custom of the Catholic Church, which undoubtedly required lights to be used on the Altar for the office of Holy Communion.

93. And the Priest standing at the North-side of the Table shall say the Lord's Prayer, with the Collect following, the people kneeling.

One Priest only is here spoken of as celebrating : there is no authority for a change of the celebrant in the course of the Service ; and only extraordinary contingencies of the gravest kind were anciently regarded as sufficient cause for such a change. Special provision is made for exceptions to this principle, in the pronouncing the Absolution by the Bishop, if officially present, and for the making the General Confession 'by one of the Ministers.' The Epistle and Gospel are also permitted to be read by Assistant Ministers, in accordance with customary usage recognised in the 24th Canon. The assistance of other Clergy may also be required for administration of the Elements.

Lay Assistants are not mentioned in this rubric, but the principle of assistance to the 'principal Minister' being recognized in the twenty-fourth Canon, there can be no objection to the ancient practice of employing clerks or choristers for other purposes than singing.

The term 'north side,' whatever was its origin (possibly the re-arrangements consequent on the transposition of the Gloria in Excelsis), acquired a meaning during the changes made in the substitution of Moveable Tables for fixed Altars about the year 1552, which determines its interpretation to exclude the north end. In those churches where the Table was placed with its long sides north and south, the Priest moved with the table, and stood at the same part of it as he had stood in the use of it as an altar, that is, at the centre of one of the long sides, though he no longer faced the same part of the Church, and now looked to the south instead of the east. But when Archbishop Laud pressed the restoration of the table to its ancient position,—a restoration which has become universal, — the question at once arose as to the position of the celebrant, and some of the

High Church clergy placed themselves at the north end of the table placed 'altarwise,' alleging that they were in this manner conforming to the rubric. They were at once met with the reply that 'side' and 'end' were not convertible terms, and it was urged that the rubric could not be complied with at all, unless the table were set with its long sides north and south. It is thus clear that the use of the end was disputed from the first, and treated as an untenable innovation. Now that the altars are universally placed so that only one of the long sides is accessible, the rubric can only be literally complied with by the celebrant standing at the northern portion of that side.

It seems, however, absurd that when the altar is restored to its place, the Priest should not be restored to his. It is further to be noted that the regarding the word 'north' rather than the word 'side,' and the placing the Priest at the north end of the altar, has the disadvantage of making the practice of the English Church unlike that of all the rest of Christendom. For all the ancient historical Churches place the celebrant in front of the altar, while the Protestant sects, even those that seat the communicants round the table, place the Minister at the centre of a side, and not at one end.

There is no direction for the Celebrant to kneel on reaching the altar, and it is contrary to general Catholic usage to do so. Any private prayers he may use then, he should say standing.

It should be remembered that the service is for the congregation, not for the Priest alone, and therefore they ought not to be detained for his personal convenience. He has not the same liberty of private devotion as the individual members of the congregation, and should carefully restrain his private devotions so as to be as short as is consistent with reverence.

It is the clear intention of the Prayer-Book that the Lord's Prayer and the whole office should be said deliberately, and sufficiently loud for the congregation to hear distinctly, so as to follow it readily. Moreover, the words of the Liturgy form an integral part of the whole sacrificial action. They are included in the oblation of praise and thanksgiving ; and, consequently, to hurry, or mutter them is, so far, to bring a blemished offering to God.

There is no direction for loudness of voice, but the words

of the office should be, as was anciently ordered, "roundly and distinctly pronounced ᵉ."

94. Then shall the Priest, turning to the people, rehearse distinctly all the TEN COMMANDMENTS ; and the people still kneeling shall, after every Commandment, ask God mercy for their transgression thereof for the time past, and grace to keep the same for the time to come, as followeth.

The Commandments were first introduced in 1552, and no rubric can be more express than this against their omission. Such omission involves also the loss of the *Kyrie*, an ancient and valuable feature of the Liturgy.

The Commandments are to be rehearsed 'turning to the people,' implying that the Priest was not standing so before.

95. Then shall follow one of these two Collects for the Queen, the Priest standing as before, and saying, Let us pray, &c.

The words 'standing as before' mean standing in the position in which the Priest was before he turned to the people to rehearse the Commandments, viz. facing eastward.

96. Then shall be said the Collect of the Day.

97. And immediately after the Collect the Priest shall read the Epistle, saying, *The Epistle* [or, *The portion of Scripture appointed for the Epistle*] *is written in the — Chapter of — beginning at the — Verse.* And the Epistle ended, he shall say, *Here endeth the Epistle.* Then shall he read the Gospel, (the people all standing up) saying, *The holy Gospel is written in the — Chapter of — beginning at the — Verse.*

98. And the Gospel ended, shall be sung or said the Creed following, the people still standing, as before.

If more collects than the collect or collects of the day be used, they must be taken from the six collects at the end of the Communion Office. If a collect be used in commemoration besides the collect of the day at Morning and Evening Prayer, it should also be used in the Communion Service.

The practice of the people sitting during the reading of the Epistle, though not prescribed in the rubric, may be justified by ancient English custom.

ᵉ " Verba Canonis *rotunde* dicantur, et distincte, nec ex festinatione retracta, nec ex diuturnitate nimis protracta."—*Decree of Herbert, Archbishop of Canterbury*, in a general synod at London, A.D. 1200 : Spelman's *Concilia*, ii. p. 123 ; John Johnson's Canons, A.-C.L., vol. ii. p. 84.

The custom of singing or saying, 'Glory be to Thee, O Lord,' before the Gospel, has been continued from ancient times, and was specially ordered in the First Prayer-Book of Edward VI. Bishop Cosin thinks that it was afterwards left out by the printers' negligence. It seems very doubtful whether ancient authority will support the saying 'Thanks be to Thee, O Lord,' or equivalent words, at the end of the Gospel, though these words were inserted in the Scottish Office.

No directions are given as to the place where the Epistle and Gospel are to be read, but one very ancient usage is, that the former is to be read at the south, the latter at the north, of the sanctuary.

From whatever part of Scripture the Epistle is taken, the words 'here endeth the Epistle' are always to be said at the end of it.

In singing or saying the Creed, it is advisable, when there are clerks, to follow the direction of the Prayer-Book of 1549, and that the Priest should sing or say alone the words ' I believe in one God,' the clerks and congregation taking up the Creed with him after those words. On bowing at the Holy Name of JESUS, the same remark may be made as on the occurrence of the Name in the Apostles' Creed.

The clergy and congregation sometimes incline the head and body at the words ' And was Incarnate.' According to ancient English custom, the inclination should be maintained until the words ' for us.' But such custom furnishes no precedent for prostration, or such exaggerated marks of reverence.

99. Then the Curate shall declare unto the people what Holy-days, or Fasting-days, are in the Week following to be observed.

This direction refers to the table of moveable and immoveable feasts together with days of fasting and abstinence, in the calendar.

And then also (if occasion be) shall notice be given of the Communion; and the Banns of Matrimony published; and Briefs, Citations, and Excommunications read. And nothing shall be proclaimed or published in the Church, during the time of Divine Service, but by the Minister: nor by him any thing, but what is prescribed in the Rules of this Book, or enjoined by the Queen, or by the Ordinary of the place.

This rubric fixes the place in the service at which notice should be given of Holy Communion, when the occasion requires.   It does not authorize the use in this place of the exhortations which are directed to be used 'after the sermon or homily ended.'

The object of the Church in the publication of Banns being publicity, it was directed to be made at a time when most people were likely to be in church, such as shortly before the Sermon. . There is some divergence between this rubric and that at the beginning of the Service for the Solemnization of Matrimony, where the Banns are directed to be published 'immediately before the sentences for the Offertory,' i.e. after the sermon, instead of before it ; and the time of publication of Banns is extended, by Stat. IV. George IV., c. 76, to the time of evening service, immediately after the 2nd lesson, if there shall be no morning service f.   It may be doubted whether a publication of Banns on Holy-days would now suffice for a legal publication, as this last-mentioned act names Sundays only.

The order for reading briefs, &c., indicates this to be the proper time for reading notices from the Bishop of intended confirmations, &c., and may perhaps be extended to cover and protect from the prohibition which follows, the announcement of dedication, harvest, and other local festivals.

The whole paragraph is connected with the Sermon, with the object of grouping together all such additions to, and interruptions of, the Office of Holy Communion.

100. Then shall follow the Sermon, or one of the Homilies already set forth, or hereafter to be set forth, by authority.

If the sermon be preached from the pulpit (for which there is no rubrical direction), and by the priest who is celebrating Holy Communion, the Chasuble should be laid aside for the function of preaching.   If the sermon be preached from the altar-steps by the celebrant the chasuble should be. retained.   If the preacher be not the celebrant, it seems to be in accordance with the Prayer-Book of 1549, and with old custom, that

---

f In most Prayer-Books printed in this century, the words 'and Banns of Matrimony published' have been omitted from this rubric ; and a corresponding alteration has been made by the printers in the first rubric in the Marriage Service, under a mistaken idea of the effect of Stat. 26 George II. cap. 33, which contained the same clause as that quoted above from the Act of 4 George IV. c. 76.

Even supposing that the words of these Acts were irreconcilable with the rubric, they did not alter the rubric.

he should wear a Surplice, as having previously taken his place in the choir, and also a hood, if a graduate.

Although the 55th Canon enjoins the use of some form of bidding the prayers before all sermons, lectures, and homilies, yet the custom may be regarded as fairly established, of beginning the sermon without any introductory form, or with a collect from the Prayer-Book, or with an invocation of the Holy Trinity, in testimony of the preacher's commission to proclaim the Gospel. The last should be announced to the people, turning the face towards them. Custom has also established, from the days at least of St. Chrysostom, the practice of ending the sermon with an ascription of praise, which may properly be pronounced turning to the East.

101. Then shall the Priest return to the Lord's Table, and begin the Offertory, saying one or more of these Sentences following, as he thinketh most convenient in his discretion.

The words 'Return to the Lord's Table' point to the Priest having left the table, either for the purpose of preaching, or to take his seat in the sedilia.

In the impoverished condition of the churches at the time of the last revision, it was well to be content that one or more of the sentences should be said by the Priest, not sung by a choir. But now that clerks and choirs have been restored to many churches, it seems reasonable that the sentences may be sung as of old, and as was prescribed in the Prayer-Book of 1549: "Where there be clerks, they shall sing one or many of the sentences above written, according to the length and shortness of the time that the people be offering."

102. Whilst these Sentences are in reading, the Deacons, Churchwardens, or other fit person appointed for that purpose, shall receive the Alms for the Poor, and other devotions of the people, in a decent bason to be provided by the Parish for that purpose; and reverently bring it to the Priest, who shall humbly present and place it upon the holy Table.

The rubric mentions but one bason, to which originally the people brought their alms, instead of putting them into the poor man's box. This one bason is wholly inefficient for making a collection by several persons, and from a large congregation; and therefore is to be used for receiving alms collected in other receptacles. It is seemly that these should be formally given out to the persons by whom the collection is to be made, and afterwards received from them in the 'decent bason' by the 'deacon, churchwarden, or other fit person appointed for that purpose,' who 'shall reverently bring it to the Priest.'

The words 'humbly present' obviously indicate some action beyond the mere placing on the Table, but do not mean a kneeling posture; for neither here nor in any other part of the Service should the Priest kneel, unless when ordered to do so.

103. And when there is a Communion, the Priest shall then place upon the Table so much Bread and Wine, as he shall think sufficient. After which done, the Priest shall say, Let us pray, &c.

The small fair linen cloth, commonly called the Veil, which is to be used after the Communion, should not be spread upon the fair white linen cloth which covers the Table, nor used to cover the Elements before the Communion.

In order to place the Bread and Wine on the Table, which must be done at this time, and not before, the Priest should have them at hand in another place. This is usually the Credence-table, or some shelf near to the altar. He places them as he did the alms, humbly, as an offering, and so much of each as he judges approximately sufficient for the communion of himself and the people. But if he should afterwards find his computation excessive—as the offering the alms and elements together is not directly connected with consecration—he is not under obligation to consecrate all that he has offered. He may, therefore, if he should think the entire contents of the Flagon likely to be required for Communion, offer the Wine in that vessel. The usage, however, of pouring a portion of the Wine into the chalice (as was directed in the Prayer-Book of 1549), and placing the chalice on the table without the flagon, has been generally maintained, though this pouring forms no part of the rubrical directions of our Liturgy, either here or at any other period of the service.

This usage is properly associated also with the primitive custom (prescribed to be used in 1549) of 'putting thereto a little pure and clean water.'

The preparatory action of mixing water with the wine (besides being connected with the original Act of Institution), was undoubtedly the custom of the time when this Church and Realm received the order of ministering the Sacrament, and it has never been prohibited in the Prayer-Book. The practice is, therefore, a performance of the Ordination vow of the English Priesthood, "so to minister the Sacraments as the Lord hath commanded, and as this Church and Realm hath received the same, according to the Commandments of God." A few drops of water are sufficient for compliance with the usage, and in no case should the quantity of water exceed one third of the whole.

If the chalice is not fitted with a cover, some substitute for a cover should be placed upon it; a small, square piece of linen, stiffened with cardboard, is sometimes used for this purpose.

It is desirable that the Priest should, as a general rule, consecrate all the Bread and Wine that he offers. And in judging the quantity, it is to be remembered that on the one hand the consecration of an excessive amount of the elements involves a serious risk of irreverence in the consumption of what remains after Communion; so on the other hand, the error of consecrating too little is to be deprecated, as necessitating a second consecration, and thereby breaking the continuity of the service.

Many such points in the service are left without direction, or with inconsistent directions, in consequence of the old Liturgical order having been so broken and distorted in the revision of 1552, that subsequent revision has been, and probably will be, unsuccessful in removing the inconsistencies.

104. If there be no alms or oblations, then shall the words [*of accepting our alms and oblations*] be left out unsaid.

105. When the Minister giveth warning for the celebration of the holy Communion, (which he shall always do upon the Sunday, or some Holyday, immediately preceding), after the Sermon or Homily ended, he shall read this Exhortation following, Dearly beloved, on, &c.

106. Or, in case he shall see the people negligent to come to the holy Communion, instead of the former, he shall use this Exhortation, Dearly beloved brethren, on, &c.

These exhortations are in anticipation of Communions on subsequent occasions, and are clearly distinct from the notice of Communion directed, in the rubric after the creed, to be given *before* the sermon, since they must come *after* the sermon. It is very difficult to say whether they should be read before or after the offertory and prayer for the Church Militant. Probably it was intended to group them generally with the sermon, without disturbing the offertory and prayer for the Church Militant.

We have here an example of inconsistency in the rubrics of

D

our Communion Office referred to in the comment on the last rubric, and which is caused by successive attempts at patching (instead of revoking) the alterations made at the revision of 1552.

These two exhortations, with the third, which is appointed for use on the occasion of Communion, form a great feature of the English rite, but are more appropriate when Communions are rare, than when they are frequent. It is, indeed, somewhat inconsistent to use a prospective exhortation on the occasion of the Communion. It is possible that the expression 'warning' may be taken to except cases where the Minister does not consider unusual mention to be imperatively necessary, and at any rate to apply only where notice is given before the sermon.

107. At the time of the celebration of the Communion, the Communicants being conveniently placed for the receiving of the holy Sacrament, the Priest shall say this Exhortation, Dearly beloved in the Lord, &c.

The rubric seems to direct a change of place to be made by the communicants, and indicates, not the general withdrawal of the rest of the congregation, but the separation of the intending communicants into a part of the church by themselves, after the precedent of the Prayer-Book of 1549, which appoints that 'they shall tarry still in the quire, or in some other convenient place nigh to the quire.'

Such a re-disposition of the congregation requires time, and would be the opportunity for the retirement of children, or other persons, who may be unable (especially when a sermon has been preached) to stay for the whole service.

The neglect of this change of place of intending communicants has introduced many difficulties connected with the attendance of those who are not prepared to communicate on the occasion, and with the orderly reception of the Communion.

This exhortation gives opportunity for intending communicants to reconsider their 'mind to come' on that occasion: it throws upon their consciences with accumulated force the individual responsibility of coming to the Lord's Table, which the relaxation of discipline, and the removal of compulsory confession, had rendered doubly important: and it being impossible that a person inadequately prepared can fulfil on the moment the requisites here enumerated for coming duly to the Lord's Table, they have no alternative but to abstain.

108. Then shall the Priest say to them that come to receive the
holy Communion, Ye that do truly, &c.

The limitation of this invitation 'to those that come to receive the Holy Communion,' is consistent with the presence
of others, and the possible retirement of some of those who
(previously to hearing the exhortation) were minded to come,
to a part of the church not occupied by communicants.

109. Then shall this general Confession be made, in the name of all those
that are minded to receive the holy Communion, by one of the Ministers ;
both he and all the people kneeling humbly upon their knees, and saying,
Almighty God, &c.

This rubric makes it clear that the Confession is primarily
intended for those who are about to communicate, though it
does not exclude others from joining in it.

With regard to the manner of making the confession, it
must be remembered that the direction that it should be made
in the name of all those that are minded to come to the Holy
Communion, was worded at a time when a considerable pro-
portion of the communicants were too illiterate to follow such
a piece of devotion by the use of a book. It was therefore
essential that their leader should say it slowly and audibly, if
they were to join in it at all. It cannot be said that this reason
has wholly disappeared now ; while even for persons of high
education, so solemn and suggestive a devotion requires all
the assistance of ample time, and facility of hearing, that they
may join in it devoutly and deliberately.

The retaining the words 'one of the Ministers,' from the
older form of the rubric, implies that if the celebrant have assistants one of them may lead the confession. And though
it may no longer be read by one of the communicant congregation (as it formerly might) still a lay-clerk at the altar is not
absolutely excluded. In any case the celebrant, even though
not leading the confession, is to kneel.

110. Then shall the Priest (or the Bishop, being present,) stand up, and
turning himself to the people, pronounce this Absolution, Almighty
God, &c.

'The Bishop' means the bishop of the diocese, or other
bishop acting in his stead. The words 'stand up,' imply that
the celebrant has been kneeling for the confession.

111. Then shall the Priest say, Hear what, &c.

112. After which the Priest shall proceed, saying, Lift up, &c.

There is authority of ancient custom (though there is no direction for so doing in the rubric) for the Priest to open his arms, and raise his hands, while pronouncing the words 'Lift up your hearts,' which are to be said facing the people.

113. Then shall the Priest turn to the Lord's Table, and say, It is very, &c.

The Priest up to this point has been 'turning to the people' in accordance with the rubric of the Absolution. He must now turn to the Lord's Table.

114. These words [*Holy Father*] must be omitted on *Trinity-Sunday*.

115. Here shall follow the Proper Preface, according to the time, if there be any specially appointed : or else immediately shall follow, Therefore, &c.

116. After each of which Prefaces shall immediately be sung or said, Therefore, &c.

A comparison with the Books of 1549 and 1552 shews that the time at which the people should join in is at the words 'Holy, &c.'

117. Then shall the Priest, kneeling down at the Lord's Table, say in the name of all them that shall receive the Communion this Prayer following, We do not presume, &c.

The Priest is assumed to be *at* the Lord's Table, *to* which he had previously turned, and is merely directed to kneel down where he is.

118. When the Priest, standing before the Table, hath so ordered the Bread and Wine, that he may with the more readiness and decency break the Bread before the people, and take the Cup into his hands, he shall say the Prayer of Consecration, as followeth, Almighty God, &c.

The expression 'standing before the Table,' is to be rightly understood by observing that the emphatic word in it is 'standing.' The intention of the framers of this direction was to put an end to the previous posture of kneeling directed in the preceding rubric, and to direct the priest to stand during the consecration. The word 'before' evidently implies a position in front of the Table, and excludes the end, whichever way the Table might be placed.

The ordering the Bread and Wine for the manual acts of consecration, might include the pouring of some of the wine from the flagon into the chalice (if not previously done); also the separation of a part of the bread from the remainder which the Priest does not now intend to consecrate, and pre-eminently the arranging conveniently the individual piece to be broken during the consecration.

The expression 'before the people' in this rubric, means simply in the presence of the people.

It was proposed by Baxter, at the Savoy Conference, to direct the Bread to be broken in the sight of the people. The framers of the rubric seem to have rejected the latter part of this proposal, and to have thought it sufficient to direct it to be done in the presence of the people, irrespective of their being able actually to see it. Any breaking the Bread at this period of the service was then a novelty, and is now peculiar to the English Liturgy. The object of the Puritans probably was to bring the ceremonial acts of the Priest in the Consecration into closer harmony with the order of our Lord's own acts and words in the Institution itself, as recorded in the Synoptic Gospels, and this part of their proposal was conceded by the bishops and the revisers, as not inconsistent with the ancient usage of *touching* the Bread at this period of the service *as if* breaking it.

The acts of reverence of the Priest, during and after consecration, according to the old English use (as may be plainly seen in the rubrics of the Sarum Missal) consisted not in bending the knee, but in bowing the head and body.

The custom of elevating the consecrated Elements was probably connected with the Jewish heave-offering, and its idea of heavenward oblation. It was directed by the most ancient Liturgies, but was expressly prohibited in the Prayer-Book of 1549. This prohibition, however, was withdrawn in 1552. The elevation cannot therefore be unlawful, though certainly it is not obligatory. The ancient rubric of Sarum gives, as a first alternative respecting the height of elevation of the chalice, that it should be raised to the height of the breast. And this, therefore, would be a sufficient compliance with ancient custom.

There seems to be no reason for pronouncing the words of Institution in a different voice from the rest of the Prayer. See note e, p. 28.

119. *Here the Priest is to take the Paten into his hands :
120. †And here to break the Bread :
121. ‡And here to lay his hand upon all the Bread.

122. ‖Here he is to take the Cup into his hand :

123. § And here to lay his hand upon every vessel (be it Chalice or Flagon) in which there is any Wine to be consecrated.

The direction of the Priest to 'lay his hand upon all the Bread and every vessel,' indicates the extreme care of the Church that none of the Bread and Wine intended for the Communicants should be overlooked in the performance of the manual acts.

It is better not to consecrate wine in the flagon (though the rubric permits it) except in the emergency of having only one chalice, and a very large number of communicants. Even in that case, a second consecration in the chalice would perhaps be preferable.

124. Then shall the Minister first receive the Communion in both kinds himself, and then proceed to deliver the same to the Bishops, Priests, and Deacons, in like manner, (if any be present,) and after that to the people also in order, into their hands, all meekly kneeling. And, when he delivereth the Bread to any one he shall say, The Body, &c.

This rubric, with the Twenty-first Canon, obliges the celebrant to receive the Communion every time that he celebrates, even if he shall do so more than once in the same day. He does so as a part of the sacrificial action, which is not complete unless a portion of the sacrifice is consumed by the offering Priest. For this reason he communicates himself, standing, as distinct from the congregation, and completing the essentials of the Sacrifice in his priestly character.

As he is not ministering to others when communicating himself, he should not speak audibly in so doing.

He is to deliver the Sacrament first of all to the Clergy assisting in the service, beginning with the Gospeller and Epistoler, in accordance with the reason assigned in the rubric of 1549 for so doing, viz. that they may be ready to help the chief minister.

The order of communicating the rest of the Clergy, and the lay congregation, would be as follows :—1. To the Metropolitan of the Province (if present). 2. To the Bishop of the Diocese (if present). 3. To other Metropolitans and Bishops (if present), in the order of their seniority of consecration respectively. 4. Priests or Deacons. 5. Lay choristers, and 6. The rest of the laity.

'In like manner' means 'in both kinds.'

'In order.' These words may refer to the distinction of sexes, as in the Clementine Liturgy [g], or more generally to the usage of taking the Sacrament to the people in their places in the choir, in contrast with the present usage of coming up to the altar-step. At all events, here is no recognition of the practice of communicating by railsful.

'Into their hands.' It was prescribed in the Prayer-Book of 1549, " that, although it be read in ancient writers that the people, many years past, received at the Priest's hands the Sacrament of the Body of Christ in their own hands, and no commandment of Christ to the contrary: yet for as much as they many times conveyed the same secretly away, kept it with them, and diversely abused it to superstition and wickedness: lest any such thing hereafter should be attempted, and that a uniformity might be used throughout the whole realm, it is thought convenient the people commonly receive the Sacrament of Christ's body in their mouths at the Priest's hand." In 1552, the manner of receiving was again put back to the use of the hands, and this has been continued since, so that the receiving in the mouth is unrubrical now [h].

Whatever be the manner of holding out the hands for the purpose of reception, the Sacrament should, in order to avoid the possibility of accident, be placed firmly and safely in the hands of the recipient, and not merely offered to be accepted with the fingers.

The words 'meekly kneeling' in this rubric exclude prostration, which is not kneeling.

The expression 'to anyone,' coupled with the use of the singular number in the address to the recipient, obliges the Priest to repeat the words of administration in delivering the Sacrament to each communicant separately.

The rubric is not clear on the point, whether the Priest

---

[g] The order of reception in the Clementine Liturgy is :—The Bishop, priests, deacons, sub-deacons, readers, singers, monastics, deaconesses, religious virgins and widows, children, all the people in order (apparently first men, and then women).

[h] The direction of St. Cyril of Jerusalem was to use the hands, making the left hand a throne for the right, and hollowing the palm of the right to receive the Body of Christ.

The fact of receiving in the hands is also noticed by Tertullian in blaming people for using for purposes which he considered unworthy the hands which they had held forth to receive God.

should give the Sacrament of the Body as soon as he has pronounced the words 'The Body of our Lord Jesus Christ,' (when the communicant may be supposed to have made an act of faith in the mystery of the Sacrament,) or whether he should give it at the end of the whole of the first sentence of administration, as he says the word 'Take.' At all events, he should not wait until he has completed the second sentence.

The words of administration should be distinctly pronounced, so as to be audible to the communicant. See note e, p. 28.

125. And the Minister that delivereth the Cup to any one shall say, The Blood, &c.

Although the word 'Minister' is used for priest in the preceding rubric and elsewhere, yet in this place it implies an important distinction between a Priest and a Deacon, the latter being forbidden by ancient Canons of the Church to deliver the Bread. And when it is declared in the Ordination of Deacons that it appertaineth to the office of a Deacon to help the Priest in the distribution of the Holy Communion, this help must be confined to the distribution of the Wine.

The rubric for the delivery of the species of Bread (directing it to be given into the hands of the communicants), seems to govern generally the administration of the Cup, though the words 'into their hands' do not occur in this rubric. Thus, the omission of these words leaves it open to the discretion of the Minister to retain his hold of the Cup while the communicant uses his hands for the purpose of guiding it. But in no case should the communicant abstain from using the hands at all, unless absolutely disabled from doing so.

It is to be noted that the directions of the rubrics on the subject of the administration of the Sacrament, are intended for the guidance of the Priest. No similar details are specified for the acts of the communicants. Hence the celebrant will use a wise discretion in not enforcing exact uniformity in the mode of reception adopted by individuals, provided it be reverent, and does not endanger the safety of the Sacrament.

There seems to be no warrant, in the English use, for making the sign of the cross with the consecrated species, paten, or chalice, in front of the communicant, at the moment of administration. At the end of the words of administration provided for the celebrant at the moment of his own Communion, in the old Sarum rite, occurs the formula '✠ In Nomine

Patris,' &c., and the sign of the Cross was directed to be made with the Body of the Lord. A similar direction was given for the chalice, which the Priest was at that moment holding in his hands. But this formula does not seem to have been used in communicating the people. If the sign of the cross had been intended to be used in the Order of Communion of 1548 (the first formula of administration in English), we may certainly presume that it would have been notified or printed as a guide, as it is in the Book of 1549, in the Prayer of Consecration, and in the Blessing of the Marriage Service. But no such guide is to be found, either there, or in any subsequent formula of administration; nor does there seem to be any ancient precedent or tradition for its use in that place. Moreover, there is a risk attending the practice, especially in the case of a large chalice nearly full of wine.

126. If the consecrated Bread or Wine be all spent before all have communicated, the Priest is to consecrate more according to the Form before prescribed : beginning at [*Our Saviour Christ in the same night*, &c.] for the blessing of the Bread; and at [*Likewise after Supper*, &c.] for the blessing of the Cup.

The necessity for consecrating more of the species of Bread can almost invariably be avoided by subdividing what is already consecrated.

127. When all have communicated, the Minister shall return to the Lord's Table, and reverently place upon it what remaineth of the consecrated Elements, covering the same with a fair linen cloth.

The direction is express to place 'what remaineth of the consecrated elements' upon the Lord's Table. The Priest is, therefore, not at liberty to consume what remains at this period of the service.

In arranging 'what remaineth of the consecrated elements,' the cover previously used, and not the paten, should be placed upon the chalice. The fair linen cloth, or veil, should be large enough to cover thoroughly the whole of both chalice and paten, when the paten is placed in front of the chalice. It should be observed, that the employment of the word 'linen' excludes a fabric of other material, such as silk or cotton.

128. Then shall the Priest say the Lord's Prayer, the people repeating after him every Petition.

129. After shall be said as followeth, O Lord and, &c.

130. Or this, Almighty and, &c.

131. Then shall be said or sung, Glory be to God, &c.

The Gloria in Excelsis, as it originally stood at the beginning of the office, in the Prayer-Book of 1549, being an opening Act of Praise, was sung by the Priest and Clerks while the people were standing.   In its altered position, it may be regarded rather as a prayer.   It seems reasonable that when it is sung in a choral celebration, the people should stand, as for an Act of Praise ; and that when it is said without music, and in a plain celebration, the people may treat it chiefly as a prayer, and so kneel.

132. Then the Priest (or Bishop if he be present) shall let them depart with this Blessing.

For the meaning of the expression 'or bishop if he be present,' see the note on rubric No. 110, p. 35.

The words 'let them depart' imply that the congregation are not to dismiss themselves previously.   Archbishop Grindal, in his injunctions to the Province of York in 1571, forbad the Minister to pause or stay between the Morning Prayer, Litany, and Communion, and directed him " to continue and say them, &c., without any intermission, to the intent that the people may continue together in prayer and hearing the word of God, and not depart out of the Church during all the time of the whole Divine Service."

The whole of the Blessing, including 'The peace of God,' &c., should be pronounced turning to the people.

The custom of reading St. John i. 1—13 aloud at the altar after the service is ended, adopted from the Roman Missal, has lately been introduced in some churches.   Such public use of this Scripture has no authority, and is in direct opposition to the ancient English custom of the Priest reciting it privately, on his way to the sacristy.

133. Collects to be said after the Offertory, when there is no Communion, every such day one or more ; and the same may be said also, as often as occasion shall serve, after the Collects either of Morning or Evening Prayer, Communion, or Litany, by the discretion of the Minister.

134. Upon the Sundays and other Holy-days (if there be no Communion) shall be said all that is appointed at the Communion, until the end of the general Prayer [*For the whole state of Christ's Church militant here in earth*] together with one or more of these Collects last before rehearsed, concluding with the Blessing.

135. And there shall be no celebration of the Lord's Supper, except there be a convenient number to communicate with the Priest, according to his discretion.

136. And if there be not above twenty persons in the Parish of discretion to receive the Communion ; yet there shall be no Communion, except four (or three at the least) communicate with the Priest.

In considering the operation of the two last rubrics, it must be remembered — 1. That the Prayer-Book gives the Curate no authority to dismiss non-communicants.—2. That the system of separating the communicants from the rest of the congregation, which underlies the rubrics in the earlier part of the office, has generally ceased to be observed. —3. That the order for signifying the names of intending communicants, at least some time the day before, has fallen into abeyance.—4. That the Curate has no opportunity of interrupting the Service for the purpose of making inquiry among the congregation of their individual intentions in this respect. The Curate, therefore, has no means of obtaining information whereon to exercise the discretion to which this rubric refers. It may happen that there being more than three or four in the church when he begins the Service, some may depart before Communion. If there be fewer, some may arrive later with the intention of communicating. In short, he cannot be certain whether or not the number of communicants be below the minimum until he has communicated himself[1].

It seems then that the utmost he can do, in order to comply with this part of the rubric, is to avoid any deliberate promoting of Solitary Communion, or nearly Solitary Communion.

In accordance with the general protest of this rubric against Solitary Communion of the Priest, he should, at all celebrations, be very careful to allow ample time for the people to present themselves for Communion, not beginning the Lord's Prayer until it is quite evident that none who intend to communicate remain without having done so.

137. And in Cathedral and Collegiate Churches, and Colleges, where there are many Priests and Deacons, they shall all receive the Communion with the Priest every Sunday at the least, except they have a reasonable cause to the contrary.

This rubric affords no ground for the opinion that Communions should not be more frequent than weekly. The direc-

[1] There seems a disposition to reduce the minimum lower than that appointed in our Rubric. The Lower House of Convocation of Canterbury have recommended its reduction to two or three, and the testimony of Bishop Torry to the ancient usage of the Scottish Church is that one was considered sufficient.

tion that the Clergy when numerous should all receive the Communion every Sunday at the least, so far from debarring them or any one else from the privilege of more frequent Communions, implies that a weekly Communion is the lowest standard in such cases. Any other principle of interpreting the words 'at the least,' in this and in the later paragraph of this rubric (where the laity are required to receive three times in the year at the least), would involve a prohibition to the laity against receiving more than three times in the year.

Bishop Cosin was of opinion that when the Church enjoined her Priests and Deacons to communicate every Sunday at least, she supposed it "ought and should be done by them oftener. And from hence was it that the Collects, Epistles, and Gospels were appointed upon the Sundays and Holy-days, and a rubric made at the beginning of the Service Book for the Collects, Epistles, and Gospels to serve all the week-days, that were used on the Sunday—that is, at any time when there is a Communion on the week-day. And, certainly, though it be no fault to read the Collects, Epistles, and Gospels either upon Sundays or week-days; yet to read them, and not to go on with the Communion, is contrary to the intent of our Church, that, if there were any company, intended a Communion every day, for the continuing of the daily sacrifice in the Church, ever used till Calvinism sprung up, and leaped over into England j."

It was a principle affirmed by Hooker and Archbishop Laud as well as by Bishop Cosin, and still later by Archbishop Sheldon in 1670, that the practice of cathedrals or mother churches was intended to be a pattern for that of parochial churches. Wherever, therefore, the Clergy form a company sufficient for communion they ought not to communicate less often than every Sunday, and may well do so oftener, even daily; and wherever a company of communicant laity desire a like privilege, they are not debarred from it by this rubric.

138. And to take away all occasion of dissension, and superstition, which any person hath or might have concerning the Bread and Wine, it shall suffice that the Bread be such as is usual to be eaten; but the best and purest Wheat Bread that conveniently may be gotten.

The words 'shall suffice' do not exclude a higher alternative, as may be seen in the rubric of administration of Bap-

tism to Infants, where they are employed in the recognition
of the validity of baptism by pouring, though it is not equally
significant with, and certainly is not exclusive of, baptism by
dipping. The true meaning is expanded in the corresponding
rubric of the Scottish Liturgy of 1637 :—" Though it be lawful to have wafer bread, it shall suffice that the bread be such
as is usual ; yet the best and purest wheat bread that conveniently may be gotten." This is more strongly expressed
by Bishop Cosin, in his comment on the similar rubric in the
Prayer-Book of 1604 :—" It is not here commanded that no
unleavened or wafer bread be used, but it is said only that
the other bread shall suffice. So that, though there was no
necessity, yet there was a liberty still reserved of using wafer
bread, which was continued in divers churches of the kingdom
and Westminster for one) till the 17th of King Charles [k].
The first use of the common bread was begun by Farel and
Viret at Geneva, in 1538, which so offended the people there,
and their neighbours at Lausanne and Berne (who had called
a synod about it), that both Farel and Viret and Calvin and
all were banished for it from the town ; where afterwards, the
wafer bread being restored, Calvin thought fit to continue it,
and so it is at this day."

The rubric insists that great care should be taken in the
selection of the bread; wherefore the Curate and Church-
wardens should not be content with the first bread that comes
to hand. Indeed, the ordinary bread of commerce scarcely
comes up to the standard of excellence and purity here required. There is no mention of any corresponding care about
the wine. But considerations of reverence obviously demand
a similar standard of excellence and purity ; and it is much
to be wished that more attention were paid to this point.
The thick and syrupy wines, commonly made up for this
sacred use, are undesirable ; on the other hand, unfermented
grape juice is not wine [1].

[k] This is A.D. 1643, the date of the total abrogation of the Prayer-Book.
[1] A distinction must, however, be drawn between the natural juice
freshly pressed from the grape which has sometimes been allowed as valid
matter for the Sacrament in cases of necessity, and the compounds now
sold as 'non-alcoholic' or 'unfermented' wines. The reason why the
former may be allowed is because it is potentially wine, and so to speak
a child-wine, and would become true wine, if given time. But the principle of wine has been killed in the latter cases, so that the artificial fluids
in question not only are not wine, but never can become wine, and are

139. And if any of the Bread and Wine remain unconsecrated, the Curate shall have it to his own use : but if any remain of that which was consecrated, it shall not be carried out of the Church, but the Priest and such other of the Communicants as he shall then call unto him, shall, immediately after the Blessing, reverently eat and drink the same.

This rubric provides for the reverent consumption of the consecrated species.

The direction to drink the Wine, as well as to eat the Bread, reverently, is imperative to compel the consumption of the Wine, as well as of the Bread. It is most desirable that care should be taken in the consecration that no more of the consecrated elements should remain than the celebrant can conveniently consume without assistance. But if it should happen that he finds it necessary to call to him other communicants for the purpose of consuming a considerable surplus, the word 'reverently' implies that they should receive it in the same posture in which they communicated.

The prohibition against carrying the unconsumed remainder of the consecrated elements out of church involves the cleansing the vessels in church. This should be done by the Priest himself. Although the Service has been concluded, the people are not required to withdraw immediately: indeed, if all left immediately after the blessing, the Priest could not call unto him any of them for the purpose of consuming the remainder of the consecrated elements.

The method of cleansing, which is really intended to ensure the entire consumption of all that remains, is not prescribed, and the word 'reverently' leaves much to the discretion of the Priest, while it certainly applies as much to his demeanour as to that of the people ᵐ."

therefore invalid matter. The statement that the Jews employ unfermented wine at the Passover, is contrary to fact. They could not have employed it in our Lord's time, because the process of arresting fermentation during so long an interval as that between the vintage and the Passover, was unknown until very lately; and the Passover cup is now naturally fermented grape wine, carefully watched from the grape to the bottle to provide against accidental admixture from without : while vinegar, itself the product of two processes of fermentation, is also used by them at the Passover.

ᵐ Note.—It is sometimes customary, with a view of scrupulously consuming the entire of the consecrated wine, to cleanse the chalice with a little wine previously to using water ; and not to pour away any water thus used until it is absolutely certain that all the consecrated species has been consumed. In the rare cases where wine has been consecrated in the flagon, that vessel must be cleansed with the same care as the chalice.

140. The Bread and Wine for the Communion shall be provided by the Curate and the Church-wardens at the charges of the Parish.

141. And note, that every Parishioner shall communicate at the least three times in the year, of which Easter to be one. And yearly at Easter every Parishioner shall reckon with the Parson, Vicar, or Curate, or his or their Deputy or Deputies; and pay to them or him all Ecclesiastical Duties, accustomably due, then and at that time to be paid.

142. After the Divine Service ended, the money given at the Offertory shall be disposed of to such pious and charitable uses, as the Minister and Church-wardens shall think fit. Wherein if they disagree, it shall be disposed of as the Ordinary shall appoint.

143. Whereas it is ordained in this Office for the Administration of the Lord's Supper, that the Communicants should receive the same kneeling; &c.

PUBLICK BAPTISM OF INFANTS,

144. The people are to be admonished, that it is most convenient that Baptism should not be administered but upon Sundays, and other Holy-days, when the most number of people come together; as well for that the Congregation there present may testify the receiving of them that be newly baptized into the number of Christ's Church; as also because in the Baptism of Infants every Man present may be put in remembrance of his own profession made to God in his Baptism. For which cause also it is expedient that Baptism be ministered in the vulgar tongue. Never-theless, (if necessity so require,) Children may be baptized upon any other day.

The main object of the rubric is that there should be a good congregation; and in preferring 'Sundays and other Holydays' to other days, because 'the most number of people' then 'come together,' the rubric implies that some come to-gether on all days, viz., to daily Morning and Evening Prayer.

145. And note, that there shall be for every Male-child to be baptized two Godfathers and one Godmother; and for every Female, one Godfather and two Godmothers.

The twenty-ninth canon of 1603 forbade parents, that is fathers, to be godfathers for their own children; but this pro-hibition was abolished by the Convocation of Canterbury in 1865, though the amended canon has not yet received the sanction of the Crown. So that the law on the subject has been for sixteen years in a state of transition, and a custom of admitting fathers to be godfathers for their children is growing up.

146. When there are Children to be baptized, the Parents shall give knowledge thereof over night, or in the morning before the beginning of Morning Prayer, to the Curate. And then the Godfathers and God-mothers, and the people with the Children, must be ready at the Font, either immediately after the last Lesson at Morning Prayer, or else immediately after the last Lesson at Evening Prayer, as the Curate by his discretion shall appoint. And the Priest coming to the Font, (which is then to be filled with pure Water,) and standing there, shall say, Hath this child, &c.

The use of the word 'Priest' here should not be taken to exclude the ministration of a Deacon in the absence of the Priest, inasmuch as the Ordination Service empowers a Deacon to baptize. But it seems to exclude the ministration of a Deacon in the presence of the Priest.

The font should be filled immediately before the Baptism, so that the water may be pure and fresh.

The official dress for the Priest is a surplice and a stole.

It is the custom of some Churches to use a shell for pouring water on the child; and it ensures the application of sufficient water. It is convenient, besides adding to the dignity of the Sacrament, that when it is ministered according to the rubric at Morning or Evening Prayer, the Priest should be attended to the font by two or more of the choir, who will hand him the shell, or napkin, or hold the book when required.

147. If they answer, *No:* Then shall the Priest proceed as followeth. Dearly beloved, &c.

148. Then shall the Priest say,
Let us pray.

At the words 'Let us pray,' the general congregation, as well as those immediately concerned in the Baptism, should kneel, the Priest continuing to stand.

The Collects, 'Almighty and Everlasting God,' and 'Almighty and Immortal God,' should be said by the Priest only, the people saying 'Amen.'

149. Then shall the people stand up, and the Priest shall say, Hear the words, &c.

150. After the Gospel is read, the Minister shall make this brief Exhortation upon the words of the Gospel. Beloved, ye hear, &c.

151. Then shall the Priest speak unto the Godfathers and Godmothers on this wise. Dearly beloved, &c.

152. Then shall the Priest say, O merciful God, &c.

In the Book of 1549 the Sign of the Cross was directed to be made in the water at the words 'Sanctify this fountain of Baptism,' which correspond to and are in substance restored by the words 'Sanctify this water' in this prayer, introduced in the revision of 1662. It seems therefore admissible to restore also the act of blessing which formerly accompanied the words now restored in substance.

153. Then the Priest shall take the Child into his hands, and shall say to the Godfathers and Godmothers,
Name this Child.
E

154. And then naming it after them (if they shall certify him that the Child may well endure it) he shall dip it in the Water discreetly and warily, saying, *N.* I baptize thee, &c.

155. But if they certify that the Child is weak, it shall suffice to pour Water upon it, saying the foresaid words. *N.* I baptize thee, &c.

Whereas in other parts of the offices of Baptism the Minister is specially directed to ask certain questions of the sponsors, but is not so directed here, it may be concluded that he is not under obligation to volunteer the inquiry whether or not the child be weak; but may baptize in the usual way by pouring, unless the sponsors request him to baptize by dipping. And practically, notice of such request should be given previously, in order that proper preparation should be made.

156. Then the Priest shall say, We receive, &c.

157. *Here the Priest shall make a Cross upon the Child's forehead.

The ancient custom was to make the cross on the child's forehead with the thumb. No water should be used.

158. Then shall the Priest say, Seeing now, &c.

Although all direction for the disposal of the child is omitted, it stands to reason that the Minister must give back the child, and care should be taken to give it to a sponsor, and not to a nurse.

159. Then shall be said, all kneeling; Our Father, &c.

160. Then shall the Priest say, We yield Thee, &c.

161. Then, all standing up, the Priest shall say to the Godfathers and Godmothers this Exhortation following. Forasmuch, &c.

162. Then shall he add and say, Ye are to, &c.

163. It is certain, by God's Word, that Children which are baptized, dying before they commit actual sin, are undoubtedly saved.

164. To take away all scruple concerning the use of the sign of the Cross in Baptism; the true explication thereof, and the just reasons for the retaining of it, may be seen in the xxxth Canon, first published in the Year MDCIV.

THE MINISTRATION OF
PRIVATE BAPTISM OF CHILDREN
IN HOUSES.

165. The Curates of every Parish shall often admonish the people, that they defer not the Baptism of their Children longer than the first or second Sunday next after their birth, or other Holy-day falling between, unless upon a great and reasonable cause, to be approved by the Curate.

166. And also they shall warn them, that without like great cause and necessity they procure not their Children to be baptized at home in their houses. But when need shall compel them so to do, then Baptism shall be administered on this fashion :

167. First, let the Minister of the Parish (or, in his absence, any other lawful Minister that can be procured) with them that are present call upon God, and say the Lord's Prayer, and so many of the Collects appointed to be said before in the Form of Publick Baptism, as the time and present exigence will suffer. And then, the Child being named by some one that is present, the Minister shall pour Water upon it, saying these words ; *N.* I baptize thee, &c.

Bishop Cosin observes : " It is not here said what shall be done in case a lawful Minister cannot be found ; or whether the child ought to be baptized again, or no, when only a midwife, or some other such, hath baptized it before." According to the ancient custom of the church, recognized and affirmed in the case of Mastin *v.* Estcott (1841), a child baptized by a layman is validly baptized. It follows, that though Baptism by any other than a Bishop, Priest, or Deacon is discouraged, and is only excusable in extreme necessity, the Sacrament should not be repeated.

In selecting the Collects for use after the Lord's Prayer, the Minister should be careful to prefer those which would not be used in the church, when the child (if it afterwards live) is brought into the church. He will therefore say (if time and present exigence will suffer) the Collects beginning,

Almighty everlasting God, who of Thy great mercy, &c.

Almighty and Immortal God, the aid of all that need, &c.

O merciful God, grant that the old Adam, &c.

Almighty ever-living God, &c., which last Collect should always be used, except in a case of extremest urgency.

168. Then, all kneeling down, the Minister shall give thanks unto God, and say, We yield Thee, &c.

169. And let them not doubt, but that the Child so baptized is lawfully and sufficiently baptized, and ought not to be baptized again.

THE RECEIVING OF THE CHILD IN THE CHURCH.

170. Yet nevertheless, if the Child, which is after this sort baptized, do afterward live, it is expedient that it be brought into the Church, to the intent that, if the Minister of the same Parish did himself baptize that Child, the Congregation may be certified of the true Form of Baptism, by him privately before used : In which case he shall say thus, I certify you, &c.

171. But if the Child were baptized by any other lawful Minister, then the Minister of the Parish, where the Child was born or christened, shall examine and try whether the Child be lawfully baptized, or no.   In which case, if those that bring any Child to the Church do answer, that the same Child is already baptized, then shall the Minister examine them further, saying, By whom, &c.

172. And if the Minister shall find by the answers of such as bring the Child, that all things were done as they ought to be ; then shall not he christen the Child again, but shall receive him as one of the flock of true christian people, saying thus, I certify you, &c.

173. After the Gospel is read, the Minister shall make this brief Exhortation upon the words of the Gospel.   Beloved, ye hear, &c.

174. Then shall the Priest demand the Name of the Child; which being by the Godfathers and Godmothers pronounced, the Minister shall say, Dost thou, &c.

175. Then the Priest shall say, We receive, &c.

176. *Here the Priest shall make a Cross upon the Child's forehead.

177. Then shall the Priest say, Seeing now, &c.

178. Then shall the Priest say, We yield Thee, &c.

179. Then, all standing up, the Minister shall make this Exhortation to the Godfathers and Godmothers.   Forasmuch, &c.

The final exhortation in the Office of Public Baptism was probably omitted here by an oversight, and should be used.

180. But if they which bring the Infant to the Church do make such uncertain answers to the Priest's questions, as that it cannot appear that the Child was baptized with *Water, In the Name of the Father, and of the Son, and of the Holy Ghost,* (which are essential parts of Baptism,) then let the Priest baptize it in the form before appointed for Publick Baptism of Infants ; saving that at the dipping of the Child in the Font, he shall use this form of words.   If thou art not, &c.

It seems very difficult, if not impossible, to combine properly the Office for Public Baptism with that for the reception of infants brought to church after having been privately baptized.   But if it must be attempted (and in large parishes it is difficult to avoid it), the Office of Public Baptism should be used, with the interposition (immediately after the reception of the infants then baptized) of the inquiries and certificates of the children privately baptized, and of their reception into the Church.   The Office of Public Baptism can be taken up again at the words, 'Seeing now, dearly beloved brethren,' and continued to the end.

THE MINISTRATION OF

BAPTISM TO SUCH AS ARE OF RIPER YEARS,

AND ABLE TO ANSWER FOR THEMSELVES.

181. When any such persons, as are of riper years, are to be baptized, timely notice shall be given to the Bishop, or whom he shall appoint for that purpose, a week before at the least, by the Parents, or some other discreet persons; that so due care may be taken for their Examination, whether they be sufficiently instructed in the Principles of the Christian Religion; and that they may be exhorted to prepare themselves with Prayers and Fasting for the receiving of this holy Sacrament.

The duty of giving notice to the Bishop is not laid upon the Curate, but upon the parents, or some other discreet persons. He is not therefore bound to give such notice.

182. And if they shall be found fit, then the Godfathers and Godmothers (the people being assembled upon the Sunday or Holy-day appointed) shall be ready to present them at the Font immediately after the second Lesson, either at Morning or Evening Prayer, as the Curate in his discretion shall think fit.

183. And standing there, the Priest shall ask, whether any of the persons here presented be baptized, or no: If they shall answer, No; then shall the Priest say thus, Dearly beloved, &c.

184. Then shall the Priest say,

Let us pray.

185. (And here all the Congregation shall kneel.)

186. Then shall the people stand up, and the Priest shall say, Hear the words, &c.

187. After which he shall say this Exhortation following. Beloved, ye hear, &c.

188. Then the Priest shall speak to the *persons* to be baptized on this wise: Well-beloved, &c.

189. Then shall the Priest demand of each of the persons to be baptized, severally, these Questions following: Dost thou, &c.

190. Then shall the Priest say, O merciful God, &c.

191. Then shall the Priest take each person to be baptized by the right hand, and placing him conveniently by the Font, according to his discretion, shall ask the Godfathers and Godmothers the Name; and then shall dip him in the water, or pour water upon him, saying, *N.* I baptize thee, &c.

If a person desire baptism by dipping, every effort should be made to provide means for the due administration of the Sacrament after the primitive manner.

192. Then shall the Priest say, We receive, &c.

193. *Here the Priest shall make a Cross upon the person's forehead.

194. Then shall the Priest say, Seeing now, dearly beloved, &c.

195. Then shall be said the Lord's Prayer, all kneeling.

196. Then, all standing up, the Priest shall use this Exhortation follow-ing ; speaking to the Godfathers and Godmothers first. Forasmuch as, &c.

197. (And then, speaking to the new baptized *persons*, he shall proceed, and say,) And as for you, &c.

198. It is expedient that every person, thus baptized, should be confirmed by the Bishop as soon after his Baptism as conveniently may be; that so he may be admitted to the holy Communion.

199. If any persons not baptized in their infancy shall be brought to be baptized before they come to years of discretion to answer for themselves ; it may suffice to use the Office for Public Baptism of Infants, or (in case of extreme danger) the Office for Private Baptism ; only changing the word [*Infant*] for [*Child* or *Person*] as occasion requireth.

200. *A CATECHISM,*
That is to say,
An Instruction to be learned of every person, before he be brought to be confirmed by the Bishop.

201. The Curate of every Parish shall diligently upon Sundays and Holy-days, after the second Lesson at Evening Prayer, openly in the Church instruct and examine so many Children of his Parish sent unto him, as he shall think convenient, in some part of this Catechism.

The time of Catechising was fixed by the 59th Canon of 1603, and by the Prayer-Book up to 1662, to be " before Evening Prayer." In 1662, this was changed to " after the Second Lesson." It must be remembered that in 1662 the Evening Prayer was said or sung in the afternoon only.

While the edifying effect of public Catechising is very great, it must be admitted that the introduction of Sunday-schools into the Church system, together with the change in the hours of Divine Service, have undoubtedly altered the conditions which rendered it necessary to provide so definite an order as this.

202. And all Fathers, Mothers, Masters, and Dames, shall cause their Children, Servants, and Apprentices, (which have not learned their Cate-chism,) to come to the Church at the time appointed, and obediently to hear, and be ordered by the Curate, until such time as they have learned all that is here appointed for them to learn.

203. So soon as Children are come to a competent age, and can say, in their Mother Tongue, the Creed, the Lord's Prayer, and the Ten Com-mandments ; and also can answer to the other Questions of this short Catechism ; they shall be brought to the Bishop. And every one shall have a Godfather, or a Godmother, as a Witness of their Confirmation.

The qualification for Confirmation, given in the rubric at the end of the Office for Public Baptism, seems to be here restricted by the addition of the words 'so soon as children are come to a competent age.' On the principle that the wider interpretation of the requisites for spiritual privileges should prevail over the narrower, this rubric should be so interpreted as not to conflict with the other. In this view, the competency here intended does not consist in having arrived at a definite age, but in understanding what they are able to repeat with their lips. It should be observed that the word 'child' used in the rubric indicates, in the language of the Canon Law, an age between seven and fourteen.

204. And whensoever the Bishop shall give knowledge for Children to be brought unto him for their Confirmation, the Curate of every Parish shall either bring, or send in writing, with his hand subscribed thereunto, the names of all such persons within his Parish, as he shall think fit to be presented to the Bishop to be confirmed. And, if the Bishop approve of them, he shall confirm them in manner following.

THE ORDER OF

CONFIRMATION,

OR LAYING ON OF HANDS UPON THOSE THAT ARE BAPTIZED AND COME TO YEARS OF DISCRETION.

205. Upon the day appointed, all that are to be then confirmed, being placed, and standing in order, before the Bishop; he (or some other Minister appointed by him) shall read this Preface following. To the end, &c.

206. Then shall the Bishop say, Do ye here, &c.

207. And every one shall audibly answer, I do.

208. Then all of them in order kneeling before the Bishop, he shall lay his hand upon the head of every one severally, saying, Defend, &c.

The word 'severally' (closely connected with the word 'saying'), and the singular number of the expression 'this thy child,' &c., indicate a distinct intention that the words should be said to each individual.

209. Then shall the Bishop say, The Lord be, &c.

210. And (all kneeling down) the Bishop shall add, Let us pray. Our Father, &c.

211. And this Collect. Almighty and, &c.

212. Then the Bishop shall bless them, saying thus, The blessing, &c.

The Blessing implies the dismissal of the congregation, and seems to exclude any idea of an address after it; for which also no place is provided during the rite, nor is any interruption to the course of the service suggested which could admit of its insertion anywhere.   However desirable it may be, it is, therefore, an unauthorized addition to the Prayer-Book.

213. And there shall none be admitted to the holy Communion, until such time as he be confirmed, or be ready and desirous to be confirmed. ·

THE FORM OF

SOLEMNIZATION OF MATRIMONY.

214. First the Banns of all that are to be married together must be published in the Church three several Sundays or Holy-days, in the time of Divine Service, immediately before the Sentences for the Offertory; the Curate saying after the accustomed manner,

On the question of the time for the Publication of Banns, see note on Rubric 99.

The rubric leaves it to the discretion of the Curate how to act, when any one rises in answer to his invitation, to declare some cause or impediment; and it is only reasonable that some words, though not set down, should be spoken by the Curate, to shew that the person has been heard.   It is perhaps advisable, having regard to the precautions directed to be taken in the later rubric touching the same matter, that the Curate, while stating that he hears the declaration, should request the objector to speak to him more fully on the matter, after the Divine service is ended; and then it is also advisable to demand that the objection should be made in writing.

215. And if the persons that are to be married dwell in divers Parishes, the Banns must be asked in both Parishes; and the Curate of the one Parish shall not solemnize Matrimony betwixt them, without a Certificate of the Banns being thrice asked, from the Curate of the other Parish.

216. At the day and time appointed for solemnization of Matrimony, the persons to be married shall come into the body of the Church with their friends and neighbours: and there standing together, the Man on the right hand, and the Woman on the left, the Priest shall say, Dearly beloved, &c.

This direction to come into the 'body of the church' is best obeyed by placing the persons to be married outside the chancel, and at the chancel-step, the Priest standing upon or above the step, and turning his face towards them.

The word 'Priest' here is to be interpreted strictly, as excluding a Deacon, in accordance with the ancient law and usage that marriage ought not to be celebrated by a Deacon. Though a marriage so celebrated would not be invalid, it is contrary to all order that a Deacon should take upon himself to pronounce the solemn benedictions of the Church contained in this rite.

217. And also, speaking unto the persons that shall be married, he shall say, I require, &c.

218. At which day of Marriage, if any man do alledge and declare any impediment, why they may not be coupled together in Matrimony, by God's Law, or the Laws of this Realm; and will be bound, and sufficient sureties with him, to the parties: or else put in a Caution (to the full value of such charges as the persons to be married do thereby sustain) to prove his allegation: then the solemnization must be deferred, until such time as the truth be tried.

219. If no impediment be alledged, then shall the Curate say unto the Man, Wilt thou have, &c.

220. The Man shall answer,

I will.

221. Then shall the Priest say unto the Woman, Wilt thou have, &c.

222. The Woman shall answer,

I will.

223. Then shall the Minister say, Who giveth, &c.

224. Then shall they give their troth to each other in this manner.

225. The Minister, receiving the Woman at her father's or friend's hands, shall cause the Man with his right hand to take the Woman by her right hand, and to say after him as followeth. I, *N.* take, &c.

Care should be taken by the Minister not to permit the father or friend who gives the woman to be married, to give the woman's hand to the man, but to receive it himself, and himself give it to the man.

226. Then shall they loose their hands; and the Woman, with her right hand taking the Man by his right hand, shall likewise say after the Minister, I, *N.* take, &c.

227. Then shall they again loose their hands; and the Man shall give unto the Woman a Ring, laying the same upon the book with the accustomed duty to the Priest and Clerk.

The order to lay the accustomed duty to the Priest and Clerk on the Book, was introduced in 1552, and this seems to be the legal opportunity for the payment of marriage-fees. It must be observed that if this rubric be complied with, the accustomed duty must be removed from the book before the Priest can conveniently proceed with the Service, though any direction for removing it is omitted in the rubric.

228. And the Priest, taking the Ring, shall deliver it unto the Man, to put it upon the fourth finger of the Woman's left hand. And the Man holding the Ring there, and taught by the Priest, shall say, With this ring, &c.

229. Then the Man leaving the Ring upon the fourth finger of the Woman's left hand, they shall both kneel down; and the Minister shall say,

Let us pray.   O Eternal God, &c.

230. Then shall the Priest join their right hands together, and say, Those whom, &c.

This is a peculiarity of the English rite, and a very solemn and important part of it.   It should, therefore, be done very carefully and accurately, and should not be obscured by any additional ceremonial, that all men may recognise the far-reaching simplicity of our Lord's prohibition of dissolution of marriage, extending to all human action, except that of the Church, whatever civil authority such other action may possess.

231. Then shall the Minister speak unto the people.   Forasmuch as, &c.

232. And the Minister shall add this Blessing.   God the Father, &c.

233. Then the Minister or Clerks, going to the Lord's Table, shall say or sing this Psalm following.   Blessed are all, &c.

It is in accordance with this rubric that the Psalm should be said or sung while going (in procession) to the Lord's Table.   The alternative, 'or Clerks,' does not affect the minister's going to the Lord's Table, as may be seen in the original rubric of the Prayer-Book of 1549, which ran 'Then shall they go into the quire, and the Ministers or Clerks shall say, or sing,' &c.   The word 'clerks' being introduced in connection with the alternative of singing, not with the going to the Lord's Table.

234. Or this Psalm.   God be merciful, &c.

235. The Psalm ended, and the Man and the Woman, kneeling before the Lord's Table, the Priest standing at the Table, and turning his face towards them, shall say, Lord, have, &c.

The Priest must obviously stand at the midst of the Holy Table, and between it and the man and woman kneeling at the steps thereof.

236. This Prayer next following shall be omitted, where the Woman is past child-bearing.   O merciful Lord, &c.

237. Then shall the Priest say, Almighty God, &c.

238. After which, if there be no Sermon declaring the duties of Man and Wife, the Minister shall read as followeth.   All ye, &c.

When the Holy Communion is celebrated at the time of a marriage, the address, if used, is to be read in the usual place of the sermon in the Communion Service.

In exercise of the liberty of choosing any suitable subject relating to the duties of man and wife, it is well to insist especially upon the indissolubility of the marriage tie.

239. It is convenient that the new-married persons should receive the holy Communion at the time of their Marriage, or at the first opportunity after their Marriage.

This rubric testifies to the intention of the Church that Matrimony should be sealed by the reception of Holy Communion. When considered in conjunction with the ancient feeling in favour of early and fasting Communion, the direction of Canon 62, that Marriages should be celebrated before twelve o'clock at noon, and the custom of styling the subsequent festivity a breakfast, all point the same way. And as Marriage is for all who desire it in the fear of God, the Church hereby assumes that all her Members are Communicants.

THE ORDER FOR

THE VISITATION OF THE SICK.

240. When any person is sick, notice shall be given thereof to the Minister of the Parish; who, coming into the sick person's house, shall say,

The direction that notice should be given to the Minister of the parish was first inserted in the Prayer-Book of 1662; indicating that he is the proper person to discharge the Priest's duty in ministering to the sick.

This office, being of a more solemn and formal character than an ordinary visit to a sick person, should be used, if possible, with proper ornaments of the Minister, such as the Surplice and Stole, or, at all events, the Stole.

241. When he cometh into the sick man's presence he shall say, kneeling down, Remember not, Lord, &c.

242. Then the Minister shall say, Let us pray.

243. Then shall the Minister exhort the sick person after this form, or other like. Dearly beloved, &c.

244. If the person visited be very sick, then the Curate may end his exhortation in this place, or else proceed. Take therefoic, &c.

245. Here the Minister shall rehearse the Articles of the Faith, saying thus, Dost thou believe, &c.

246. The sick person shall answer, All this, &c.

247. Then shall the Minister examine whether he repent him truly of his sins, and be in charity with all the world ; exhorting him to forgive, from the bottom of his heart, all persons that have offended him ; and if he hath offended any other, to ask them forgiveness ; and where he hath done injury or wrong to any man, that he make amends to the uttermost of his power.   And if he hath not before disposed of his goods, let him then be admonished to make his Will, and to declare his Debts, what he oweth, and what is owing unto him ; for the better discharging of his conscience, and the quietness of his Executors.   But men should often be put in remembrance to take order for the settling of their temporal estates, whilst they are in health.

248. These words before rehearsed may be said before the Minister begin his Prayer, as he shall see cause.

249. The Minister should not omit earnestly to move such sick persons as are of ability to be liberal to the poor.

In obeying this explicit direction, the Minister must consider that hasty and inconsiderate almsgiving, especially by will, such as bequeathing doles to the inhabitants of particular places, has been productive of much evil. He must also be careful not to advise acts of liberality which are disproportionate to the ability of the sick person, or illegal (as, e.g., in contravention of the Mortmain Acts) ; and in general he will do well to refrain from suggesting any special objects of benevolence.

When the sick person prepares an offering of alms, and is afterwards communicated, his alms may well be offered after the Gospel, in the Office for the Communion of the Sick.

250. Here shall the sick person be moved to make a special Confession of his sins, if he feel his conscience troubled with any weighty matter. After which Confession, the Priest shall absolve him (if he humbly and heartily desire it) after this sort.

The significant introduction in the last revision of this direction to 'move' the sick person to make a special confession of his sins, recalls the fact that the practice of confession had then been interrupted for many years, and required exertion for its revival. In 'moving' the sick person, is included instruction upon the nature and details of sins, as well as help to discover them, such as the suggestion of questions on the Commandments, Baptismal obligations, marriage vows, &c. The expression 'special confession' does not mean a *partial* confession, but a confession which goes into *detail ;* and the

Priest should not absolve the sick person unless his confession comprehends, besides the weighty matter which had immediately prompted it, all matters which ought to press upon his conscience, and can be recalled to mind by his utmost efforts.

The words ' if he humbly and heartily desire it,' do not refer to the expression of the penitent's desire for absolution as a positive condition of his receiving it, but denote a state of mind suitable to receiving it, and the absence whereof, if manifested, would justify the priest in withholding absolution.

'After this sort' means *in this form,* and is an express direction to use the form of absolution which then follows. The form here prescribed is employed in this office as being the usual form of private absolution in all cases, and is recognised as such in the Prayer-Book of 1549, where it is enjoined for universal private use. Neither does it contain any such allusion to sickness or weakness of body, or to unlikelihood of recovery, as would render it inappropriate for persons in health.

251. And then the Priest shall say the Collect following. O most merciful, &c.

252. Then shall the Minister say this Psalm. In Thee, O Lord, &c.

253. Adding this. O Saviour, &c.

254. Then shall the Minister say, The Almighty Lord, &c.

255. And after that shall say, Unto God's, &c.

256. A Prayer for a sick Child. O Almighty God, &c.

257. A Prayer for a sick Person, when there appeareth small hope of recovery. O Father of mercies, &c.

258. A commendatory Prayer for a sick person at the point of departure. O Almighty God, &c.

259. A Prayer for persons troubled in mind or in conscience. O Blessed Lord, &c.

THE

COMMUNION OF THE SICK.

260. Forasmuch as all mortal men be subject to many sudden perils, diseases, and sicknesses, and ever uncertain what time they shall depart out of this life; therefore, to the intent they may be always in a readiness to die, whensoever it shall please Almighty God to call them, the Curates shall diligently from time to time (but especially in the time of pestilence, or other infectious sickness) exhort their Parishioners to the often receiving

of the holy Communion of the Body and Blood of our Saviour Christ, when it shall be publickly administered in the Church; that so doing, they may, in case of sudden visitation, have the less cause to be disquieted for lack of the same.

261. But if the sick person be not able to come to the Church, and yet is desirous to receive the Communion in his house : then he must give timely notice to the Curate, signifying also how many there are to communicate with him, (which shall be three, or two at the least,) and having a convenient place in the sick man's house, with all things necessary so prepared, that the Curate may reverently minister, he shall there celebrate the holy Communion, beginning with the Collect, Epistle, and Gospel, here following.

The opening direction of this rubric evidently contemplates regular and frequent opportunities of access to the public administration of the Holy Communion in church, such as would suffice for times of great danger and distress ; and therefore implies frequent celebrations as a permanent system. Otherwise, it would be mere hypocrisy to exhort men to the often receiving thereof, and that, not only in time of pestilence, &c., but generally and habitually. A special order for those not able to come to church was unknown in the Church until 1549. Previously to that date no provision was made for their case, except by the reservation of some of the Blessed Sacrament from the open Communion in the church, and its conveyance to them afterwards ; and in the Book of 1549, the order was introduced for use on such days as there was no open Communion in church. The word 'reverently' may be best satisfied by as near an approximation to the ceremonial of the open Communion in the church as can be attained, in regard of the ornaments of the Church and Minister. In addition to the usual vessels for the celebration of the Holy Communion, the Minister will do well to provide himself with a spoon, for the administration of the species of Wine to very feeble persons.

Cases will occur where the difficulty of swallowing even very small quantities of either the Bread or the Wine is almost insuperable. Administration in both kinds may, in some of these cases, be still attained by placing a minute particle of the Bread in the spoon with some of the Wine, or conversely by touching the Wine in the cup with the corner of the piece of Bread which is to be given to the sick person.

In cases of long infirmity, as of bedridden people without acute illness, the analogy of the Office of Private Baptism would seem to hold good, and to admit of the introduction of the other parts of the Order of Holy Communion, besides those appointed for the Communion of the Sick.

262. After which the Priest shall proceed according to the form before prescribed for the holy Communion, beginning at these words [*Ye that do truly*, &c.]

263. At the time of the distribution of the holy Sacrament, the Priest shall first receive the Communion himself, and after minister unto them that are appointed to communicate with the sick, and last of all to the sick person.

264. But if a man, either by reason of extremity of sickness, or for want of warning in due time to the Curate, or for lack of company to receive with him, or by any other just impediment, do not receive the Sacrament of Christ's Body and Blood, the Curate shall instruct him, that if he do truly repent him of his sins, and stedfastly believe that Jesus Christ hath suffered death upon the Cross for him, and shed his Blood for his redemption, earnestly remembering the benefits he hath thereby, and giving him hearty thanks therefore, he doth eat and drink the Body and Blood of our Saviour Christ profitably to his Soul's health, although he do not receive the Sacrament with his mouth.

The instruction ordered to be given to the sick man, under certain circumstances, of unavoidable impediment to his receiving the Sacrament of Christ's Body and Blood 'that he nevertheless doth eat and drink Christ's Body and Blood,' must be understood to mean that physical incapacity to eat and drink does not cut off the sick man from the benefits of Holy Communion. But this rubric does not justify any wilful or habitual neglect of receiving the Sacrament itself.

265. When the sick person is visited, and receiveth the holy Communion all at one time, then the Priest, for more expedition, shall cut off the form of the Visitation at the Psalm [*In thee, O Lord, have I put my trust*, &c.] and go straight to the Communion.

266. In the time of the Plague, Sweat, or such other like contagious times of sickness or diseases, when none of the Parish or neighbours can be gotten to communicate with the sick in their houses, for fear of the infection, upon special request of the diseased, the Minister may only communicate with him.

THE ORDER FOR
THE BURIAL OF THE DEAD.

267. Here is to be noted, that the Office ensuing is not to be used for any that die unbaptized, or excommunicate, or have laid violent hands upon themselves.

This order was adapted for a state of society in which the Parish Priest was intimately acquainted with the circumstances of every deceased person who was brought to be buried. Under the altered conditions of the present day, the officiating Priest being often in ignorance of the lives and deaths of those over whom he has to perform the office of the Church, has no power of inquiry given him, nor any authority to delay a burial for the purpose of making such inquiry. He is, therefore, not obliged to seek for these exceptions, nor to infer their existence, from his own previous knowledge of the matter, unless that knowledge be very clear, and founded upon certain evidence.

The exception of the unbaptized does not apply to those who have received Lay or Schismatical Baptism, provided the proper matter and form had been used.

The word 'excommunicate' means under formal sentence of excommunication passed by a competent Spiritual Court. It is equivalent to the words 'denounced excommunicated' in Canon 68. Even those who are 'ipso facto excommunicated,' by virtue of Canons 2 to 9, are not technically 'excommunicate,' until after trial and sentence, the words 'ipso facto' having in English Canon Law a special technical meaning, viz. that the offence cannot be punished by a sentence of less severity.

268. The Priest and Clerks meeting the Corpse at the entrance of the Churchyard, and going before it, either into the Church, or towards the Grave, shall say, or sing, I am the Resurrection, &c.

The alternative of saying the sentences going towards the grave is intended to meet exceptional cases of apprehended infection, when it might be dangerous to bring the body into the church. No distinction of spiritual condition was contemplated. It is clearly the general intention of the revisers of 1662 that the corpse should in ordinary cases be brought first into the church. But when under special circumstances it has been taken from the entrance of the churchyard directly to the grave, there seems no reason why the people should not return to the church after the interment, for the reading the Psalms and Lesson, as was expressly provided in the Prayer-Book of 1549.   .

When the corpse is taken first to a church, and afterwards to a distant cemetery, the part of the service which follows the Lesson being necessarily reserved for use at the grave, the previous part, i.e. the Sentences, Psalms, and Lesson, which were said at the church, should not be repeated at the grave.

269. After they are come into the Church, shall be read one or both of these Psalms following. I said, &c., *and* Lord, Thou hast been, &c.

When the corpse is brought into the church, it is usually placed in the Nave. In the burial of a Priest it would seem decorous to place the corpse in the Chancel. In either case the feet should be towards the east.

The place of the officiating Priest, in reading the Psalms and Lesson, is not specified. Sometimes it is the custom to stand at the feet of the corpse (when it is placed near the Chancel), so that the congregation may be in front of the Priest, but usually he would occupy 'the accustomed place.' The 90th Psalm seems the most appropriate for burial of an aged person.

270. Then shall follow the Lesson taken out of the fifteenth Chapter of the former Epistle of Saint Paul to the Corinthians.

271. When they come to the Grave, while the Corpse is made ready to be laid into the earth, the Priest shall say, or the Priest and Clerks shall sing : Man that is born, &c.

In the Prayer-Book of 1549 the casting the earth upon the body was directed to be done by the Priest, with the words, 'I commend thy soul to God the Father Almighty.' This action was transferred from the Priest to 'some standing by,' when those words were omitted in 1552. The present rubric seems to direct that any one else is to perform the act. If done, as it usually is, by the Parish Clerk, or other inferior Church official, there is more dignity in it than if done by an unofficial person.

If there is a celebration of Holy Communion at the time of a burial, it is a separate service, and the celebrant must remember that the use of any Collect, Epistle, and Gospel, except the one for the day, is very difficult to justify as being in accordance with the rubrics of either service. See Rubric 6.

272. Then, while the earth shall be cast upon the Body by some standing by, the Priest shall say, Forasmuch as it hath, &c.

273. Then shall be said or sung, I heard a voice, &c.

274. Then the Priest shall say, Lord, have mercy, &c.

THE

THANKSGIVING OF WOMEN AFTER CHILD-BIRTH,

COMMONLY CALLED,

THE CHURCHING OF WOMEN.

275. The Woman, at the usual time after her Delivery, shall come into the Church decently apparelled, and there shall kneel down in some convenient place, as hath been accustomed, or as the Ordinary shall direct : And then the Priest shall say unto her, Forasmuch, &c.

By the direction that the woman should be decently apparelled, it was originally meant that she should be veiled. This was part of the general practice of her being (in the words of the Bishops at the Savoy Conference), 'perspicuous to the whole congregation.' And although the custom of veiling cannot be revived, yet its principle of marking the individual should be borne in mind in the arrangement of the Service, as e.g. placing the woman in a special place.

The convenient or proper place in which the woman was to kneel, was 'near the church door' in the ancient English use, 'near the choir door' in the Prayer-Book of 1549, 'nigh unto the place where the Table standeth' in the book of 1552. The words 'as hath been accustomed' refer to the one of these usages which has survived, and been adhered to, in any old church. The place at the altar rails was approved by the Bishops at the Savoy Conference, in regard of the offering she is there to make. The Priest, in all cases, should stand by her—i.e. near to, and in front of, her.

He is to say to her the Address and the Psalm. The congregation should not join in the latter. Care must be taken not to replace from an ordinary Psalter the verses omitted from the 116th Psalm.

· In cases where the new-born child has died, it is better to use the 116th Psalm.

276. (Then shall the Priest say the cxvith Psalm,)

277. Or *Psalm cxxvii.*

278. Then the Priest shall say,

Let us pray. Lord, have mercy, &c.

The Priest may at this point properly turn to look eastward.

279. The Woman, that cometh to give her Thanks, must offer accustomed Offerings; and, if there be a Communion, it is convenient that she receive the holy Communion.

The Service is intentionally concluded without a blessing, which it is wrong to insert. The suggestion of the woman's receiving the Holy Communion is aided by the incompleteness of the Service ending abruptly with the Thanksgiving.

With regard to the time of the Service, there is no express direction, provided that a congregation may be reasonably expected.

The offering of the woman is connected with her receiving the Holy Communion, and should be made in that Service, if she comes to it. In all cases, it is well that it should be formally received by the Priest or an assistant, in an alms-bag or bason, and presented by the Priest on the Altar.

It is to be observed that no mention is made of the condition of the woman, as being in wedlock or not. When it was objected at the Savoy Conference that some profession of humiliation ought to be required of an unmarried or profligate woman before she was admitted to the privilege of thanksgiving, the Bishops replied, "that such a woman should do her penance before she was churched."

If the Priest, therefore, be privately cognizant of the penance of such a woman, he is bound to admit her to the Service, without requiring public profession of her humiliation. Without such cognizance he could hardly admit such a woman to a Service which expressly implies access to Communion.

A COMMINATION,

OR DENOUNCING OF GOD'S ANGER AND JUDGEMENTS AGAINST SINNERS,

With certain Prayers to be used on the First Day of Lent, and at other Times, as the Ordinary shall appoint.

280. After Morning Prayer, the Litany ended according to the accustomed manner, the Priest shall, in the Reading-Pew or Pulpit, say, Brethren, &c.

The 51st Psalm is directed to be said, not 'said or sung.' Singing, therefore, appears to be excluded, as it was, in the similar place in the old English Office, by the direction to say the Psalm *sine notâ*.

281. And the people shall answer and say, Amen.

282. Then shall they all kneel upon their knees, and the Priest and Clerks kneeling (in the place where they are accustomed to say the Litany) shall say this Psalm.   Have mercy upon me, &c.

283. Then shall the people say this that followeth, after the Minister. Turn Thou us, &c.

284. Then the Minister alone shall say, The Lord bless us, &c.

www.ingramcontent.com/pod-product-compliance
Lightning Source LLC
Chambersburg PA
CBHW020236090426
42735CB00010B/1721